The Exploding Whale
and Other Remarkable Stories from the Evening News

Paul Linnman

WestWinds Press®

For my sons—Darin, Jason, Ryan, and Adam—with thanks
for all of the laughs. About the exploding whale and other things.
—Paul Linnman

Text © 2003 by Paul Linnman
Whalesong, © 1998 by Daniel M. Kanemoto/Ex Mortis Films LLC, appears with permission
Dave Barry's column "Moby Yuck" © 1990 by *Miami Herald*, appears with permission
Exploding whale stills, by Doug Brazil, © 1970 by KATU-TV, appear with permission

WestWinds Press®
An imprint of Graphic Arts Center Publishing Company
P.O. Box 10306, Portland, Oregon 97296-0306
503/226-2402; www.gacpc.com

Library of Congress Cataloging-in-Publication Data
Linnman, Paul, 1947-
  The exploding whale : and other remarkable stories from the evening news /
by Paul Linnman ; photography by Doug Brazil.
      p. cm.
  ISBN 1-55868-743-2
  1. Linnman, Paul, 1947-   2. Television journalists—United States—Biography.
I. Brazil, Doug. II. Title.
PN4874.L447A3 2003
070.92—dc22   2003019320

President: Charles M. Hopkins
Associate Publisher: Douglas A. Pfeiffer
Editorial Staff: Tricia Brown, Jean Andrews, Kathy Howard, Jean Bond-Slaughter
Editor: Timothy W. Frew
Production Staff: Richard L. Owsiany, Susan Dupere
Design: *Cover*—Elizabeth Watson; *Interior*—Constance Bollen

Printed in the United States of America

Contents

Preface / 5

CHAPTER ONE
We're Getting Paid for This? / 9

CHAPTER TWO
Getting There / 13

CHAPTER THREE
Meanwhile, Back at the Whale... / 19

CHAPTER FOUR
Video Death Rangers / 25

CHAPTER FIVE
Pregnant Olympians and Prison Riots / 31

CHAPTER SIX
And Now Some Other Amazing Mammals / 42

CHAPTER SEVEN
What Is It and What Killed It? / 55

CHAPTER EIGHT
What Happens When You Don't Quit / 63

CHAPTER NINE
Having a Blast at the Beach / 71

CHAPTER TEN
Mind over Matter / 80

CHAPTER ELEVEN
Professional Blubbering / 90

CHAPTER TWELVE
Airplanes, Race Cars, and Cartoons / 97

CHAPTER THIRTEEN
How It All Began / 108

CHAPTER FOURTEEN
Really Playing It as It Lies / 118

CHAPTER FIFTEEN
Sam Donaldson and
Someone Named Murphy / 128

CHAPTER SIXTEEN
Kids, Music, Movies, and Cancer / 135

CHAPTER SEVENTEEN
Three Guys Who Kept the Whale Alive / 145

CHAPTER EIGHTEEN
Toilet-Paper Philanthropy / 152

CHAPTER NINETEEN
Where the Arts and Marine Biology Meet / 160

CHAPTER TWENTY
Giving Kids Their Own Legs / 172

CHAPTER TWENTY-ONE
The Two Who Blew / 183

CHAPTER TWENTY-TWO
What We Can Learn from Mammals / 193

CHAPTER TWENTY-THREE
Who We Can Really Blame for All of This / 209

CHAPTER TWENTY-FOUR
Enough Is Enough / 215

Acknowledgments / 223

Preface

NOT LONG AGO on a television talk show in Portland I interviewed a young woman about a book she had written. It was the story of the woman's extremely painful childhood. Among other things, she had lived in thirty different foster homes by the time she was thirteen.

Since most of us would probably try to put such a past behind us and forget it as best we could, I asked her why she decided to write a book about it. She said she had reached a point after having thought about her own story so much that she needed to "give it over."

"'I had to find a different container for it' is the best way I can explain it," she said. "And I thought the best way to do that was to write about it. It's like, set it in a basket, in an ocean, and let it find where it needs to go. And let it help others along the way."

I don't mean to imply that what follows is comparable in any way to what this young woman experienced in her tragic childhood years— it is not. But prior to that interview, I had never heard anyone so simply put into words what I had long felt about this story—that it needed to be given over, put in a different container, and sent on its way. The young author had captured my feelings precisely.

I have lived with this story for three and a half decades, since the very early days of my career as a journalist. I have been asked about it nearly every day. I have seen it travel around the world in many forms, carried on the lips—and on the home television screens—of untold thousands, no, by now, millions. I have read what scores of other reporters have written about it, and I have read what media critics have written about my own writing about it.

I have stopped counting the number of times a different branch of government or another major corporation has discovered the story and put it to its own use.

And maybe because I have been the target of unceasing, good-natured ribbing about it, I'm no longer surprised when I hear of a governor or a captain of industry somewhere who routinely watches his or her own video copy of the story for a laugh or two after a long, stressful day. Many people find it hilarious.

I'm aware of all of this and more, as this book attempts to chronicle. But I don't pretend to fully comprehend why this single story, unlike the thousands of others I've covered in my career, the vast majority of which were of much greater significance, has taken on a global life of its own.

One of my favorite adages—and I believe it was originally a Jewish admonition—suggests that the best way to make God laugh is to tell Him your plans for the future. On that fall day back in 1970, I had no idea that this one incident and how I reported on it would stay with me in so many ways for so long into the future.

The television station I worked for had asked me to report on something, which seemed odd yet simple: the disposal of a dead whale that had washed up on an Oregon beach. I covered the event, which admittedly turned out to be more bizarre than I had expected, but still remember thinking at the time, that's that, what's the next assignment? It's how most reporters think—don't ask them what they covered yesterday, or about any other "old" news.

Conversely, in my work I have met and reported on innumerable individuals who I found to be incredibly memorable. In almost all cases, their stories were inspiring—my favorite subjects being ordinary people who were doing extraordinary things in their lives, often to the benefit of many others. In one series alone, I reported on 1,215 such people—regularly convincing producers to somehow find room for these "good news" stories in their nightly newscasts, time that otherwise would be given to more doom and gloom.

The irony of it is that nobody ever, ever asks me about any of those subjects. No one in the checkout line inquires about the businessman I reported on who sold his house and quit his job to build orphanages in Romania, or the woman who adopted a house full of severely handicapped children. No, when someone directs a question or comment to me about my reporting, it's going to have the whale in it, guaranteed.

It has been that way for years, and it's brought me to the point where I feel compelled to "give it over." What follows is the entire story of Oregon's now infamous "exploding whale," in as great a detail as I can possibly recall after all of this time. While the subject has been elevated to urban legend status in various places, many subsequent accounts of the event have been embellished and sensationalized. This, as best as I can tell it, is the true story.

However, I can't in good conscience tell that story without sharing, side-by-side with it, the stories of some subjects I found to be all the more remarkable. My original intention was to title this book, "The Exploding Whale and Other Amazing Mammals," but the publishers were rightly concerned that would be misleading, that readers might expect it to be full of stories about other whales and dolphins and what not. Still, it's my hope that the stories of these other "amazing mammals" will be received with something akin to the same kind of interest "the whale" has generated for so long.

For good measure, I've also thrown in an "inside television news" anecdote or two, as well as a few thoughts on the nature of the TV news business, an odd beast at the very least. Like the young author who wrote about her childhood, I set these stories in a new container and let them find where they need to go. And who knows, maybe somehow they will help others along the way.

Paul Linnman
September 2003
Portland, Oregon

CHAPTER ONE

We're Getting Paid for This?

Just occasionally you find yourself in an odd situation.
You get into it by degrees and in the most natural
way, but, when you are right in the midst of it, you are
suddenly astonished and ask yourself how in the world
it all came about.

—*Thor Heyerdahl*, Kon-Tiki, *1951*

WE COULD SMELL IT the moment we stepped from the car. Not anything recognizable, just this incredible stench, which grew stronger as we walked up the sand dune trail heading toward the beach. Was it my imagination, or was it also putting a taste in my mouth, something completely foreign to the fresh salt air one normally enjoys at the beach? This was on the order of spoiled meat, only stronger.

Funny thing about that smell: I would never again think of this day, or what was about to happen, without the horrible odor returning instantly to my memory. Just as I've never been able to adequately describe it to others, I fear I will never be able to completely escape it.

I glanced over at Doug, my photographer, as we made our way up the dune through the deep, dry sand, both of us loaded down with cameras, tripod, and assorted gear. We were the same age, twenty-three, and relative newcomers to the television news business, but we had already covered several stories together and liked our jobs a lot.

We'd also been developing a nonverbal communication on our assignments, so when Doug looked back at me with arched eyebrows and a slight grin, I gave him an understanding nod. We were a couple of wise guys embarking on another curious adventure, and we were being paid by a Portland television station to do it.

The mid-morning sun broke through high overcast as we paused at the top of the dune to survey the beach below and get our first look at what was stinking up the place. The dead, forty-five-foot, eight-ton whale was easy to spot, lying in isolation like a long, high rock on the beach. It had washed up three days before, and now with the tide out, rested about fifty yards above the breakers. We could also see several men—one using a small bulldozer—moving around the carcass, busy as construction workers on a job site. Man, I thought, it must really stink down there.

It was an otherwise typical fall day on the Southern Oregon Coast near the town of Florence, a pleasant little community spread along Highway 101. The climate on the South Coast is mild, and because Florence is at the head of the forty-two-mile-long Oregon Dunes Recreation Area, it's a popular place with tourists.

Doug and I looked at the whale for a little longer before resuming our hike to the beach.

"Isn't one of us supposed to say, 'Thar she blows?' or something?" Doug asked, but I didn't answer. I was busy thinking about what was actually happening here, and what kind of information I needed to make a story out of it.

I studied journalism in college, but the truth was no one had ever instructed me in how to "cover" a story. All of those classroom discussions were more about writing and the ordering of facts *after* all of the questions had been asked, not how to ask what of whom when you're there. And since I only studied print journalism, I hadn't learned a thing about putting pictures with words to make a story for television.

The film was Doug's job—he generally just shot everything he thought might be needed, sometimes with some direction from me if he missed something—but as the reporter and producer of our stories, it was ultimately my job to piece the pictures and words together in a nice, tight package.

It had gone okay so far in a couple of years of reporting, and I guess I'd learned to do what Doug did—get all of the information I thought I might need, and hope that I wouldn't be missing anything when I'm back at my typewriter in the newsroom. It wasn't "rocket surgery," Doug and I liked to joke, but still I wondered if real reporters used little tricks or techniques that I didn't know about. Or did everyone learn how to do his or her job just by doing it?

Our assignment that day, Thursday, November 12, 1970, was to cover the disposal of a dead whale for the five o'clock news, which sounded easy enough, if of questionable news value—but this thing had an odd twist to it. My boss had learned that the whale was going to be blown up with dynamite.

"The wire service says they're going to blast that baby to smithereens," Pat Wilkins, the news director at KATU-TV, explained to us that morning. "Why don't you guys fly down there and see what happens." Leaving Pat's office, Doug and I gave each other the look. This might be fun.

To begin with, we'd never flown anywhere to cover a story before, which seemed so big time, like what network crews do. We still acted as if it was strictly routine during the one-hour flight to the coast in our single-engine charter, and talked about how strange it seemed that anyone would blow up a whale. Carting it off to the dump—maybe burying it—seemed more logical.

Before we left the newsroom that morning, Pat Wilkins had explained to us that the State Highway Division, under the Oregon Department of Transportation, was in charge of the whale removal job. The reason was that in the days before Highway 101, motorists traveled the Oregon Coast by driving up and down the beaches, taking ferries over the many rivers that flowed into the Pacific Ocean from the Coast Range. In 1913, Oregon Governor Oswald West declared the state's beaches to be public thoroughfares and ordered the Highway Division to keep them free of debris. This apparently included dead whales.

Doug and I borrowed a car from the man who managed the Florence airport and drove the short distance out South Jetty Road to the beach. We were both excited about what we were about to witness, but had no real idea of what to expect.

"I mean, I was sort of wondering why we were down there to begin with," Doug would recall several years later, "not realizing the size of the whale or exactly what they'd try to do to it. Not having seen an exploding whale before, I had no anticipation of what it would be like, I mean absolutely none."

There was certainly no way we could have known upon arriving in this peaceful community on the Oregon Coast that, in a few hours, both of us would be running for our lives, trying to escape the heavy and potentially lethal pieces of whale blubber that rained from the sky. Nor could we anticipate that this one news story would be with us forever and, in some ways, define our careers.

And how could we ever have foreseen that for the next three decades and more, people around the world—individuals, government organizations, and officials of all kinds—would want us to tell them about Oregon's exploding whale? Was it true, they demanded to know, or was this another of those "urban legends?" And if it had actually happened, they were always quick to ask, could we see the video, too?

The smell grew worse as we got closer to the beach, and I wondered just how bad it might get when the decomposing whale was blown open with dynamite. But then another thought flashed into my mind: No. They wouldn't really do that, would they? Who would blow up a whale?

CHAPTER TWO

Getting There

Literature deals with the ordinary, the unusual;
and extraordinary things belong to journalism.
—*James Joyce*

A HIGH SCHOOL ENGLISH TEACHER and a bad memory were responsible for getting me into television news, and ultimately, to the whale.

I grew up in a post–World War II Southwest Portland housing
development called Vermont Hills. My parents—dad a heavy-drinking
insurance man who played trumpet in jazz bands on the weekends,
mom a housewife who never learned to drive and subsequently seldom
left the house—had very little money, but somehow managed to send
my older brother and sister and me to a parochial grade school.

The academic competition at St. Thomas More—fueled by the
not-so-gentle prodding from the Sisters of the Holy Names—
somehow earned me straight As for eight years. But neither the
learning nor the good grades came easy, and I could never seem to hide
from the good sisters (which was my goal), even in a classroom of fifty
kids, which was our baby-boomer class size all eight years. The other
forty-nine kids seemed to take right to whatever was being taught,
while I struggled and developed a tremendous dislike of school.

After convincing my parents to let me attend a public high school,
I was thrilled to discover that my teachers at Woodrow Wilson High,
at least compared to the nuns, didn't much care what kind of grades I
got. I skated by with Cs—good enough to keep me on the baseball and

football teams—and became yet another class clown, clearly disinterested in what was being taught and good-naturedly antagonistic to anyone who tried to teach it.

Much later in life—and I guess it was working as a reporter as much as anything else that brought it about—I did come to love learning. And even though I now look back on my mostly wasted school years with considerable regret, I realize that there must have been some learning going on, a tribute to the teachers who didn't buy my "disinterested jock" act.

Two of my coaches, Vern Marshall and Bob McFarlane, taught me the most—in the main, how to behave in life, how to get along with others, and how to play the game, whether you won or lost. This stuff proved more useful in the long run than anything I was taught in class, which I believe proves the importance of school athletic programs. School sports always and everywhere seem to be on the brink of losing their funding. But for countless numbers of school kids—and I was one of them—coaches may be the most important teachers of all.

Even so, for me there was a defining moment in the classroom that more than anything else determined my career direction. I took sophomore English from a much-loved teacher named Troy Horton, a nonconformist who won over his students from the very start with an offbeat sense of humor and an ability to earn everyone's respect simply by being himself.

One day in class, as Mr. Horton was returning some papers we had written, I sat at my desk openly reading *MAD Magazine*, doing my wise guy act and hoping to get noticed for it. Mr. Horton didn't even stop, but as he dropped my paper on my desk from about shoulder height, he mumbled something in his funny, offbeat way, which would stay with me for a long time to come. He said, "It's too bad you don't give a shit, Linnman, because I think you can write a little."

That was it—not much of an inspirational speech—but definitely enough to get my attention and start me thinking seriously about writing. I gravitated toward journalism, and the following year began writing for the school paper, *The Statesman*, becoming its sports editor the year after that. More importantly, I'd finally found something in school that I actually enjoyed and could do with relative ease. Nothing, as the saying goes, succeeds like success.

And there were other small rewards. Because most of my early articles for the paper didn't carry a byline, it took my sports teammates a while to figure out why I was regularly written about in the school paper, even after lackluster performances in games. I just felt that getting to write a paragraph or two about myself was, well, kind of my pay. Working on the paper also got me out of class a lot to go "cover" something, whether I had an actual assignment or not. My first journalistic perk!

But it was Mr. Horton's encouragement that got me going, and it's been my mission and joy in the years since, when speaking to educators, to remind them of the lesson learned by one disinterested student at Portland's Wilson High School. Forget worrying about class sizes, outdated textbooks, and the kids you might be losing. A few encouraging words, perhaps having absolutely nothing to do with the subject being taught, can have life-changing results.

After high school, I spent two terms bringing my grades up at Multnomah Junior College in Portland, so I could get into a four-year college. Since most everyone else had left town for more prestigious institutions of learning, we Multnomah students took to calling our sorry little JC (long since out of business) "MIT," for "Multnomah In Town." I honestly believe that I got my first job at a newspaper, the Portland *Oregonian*, because when asked in an interview by the circulation manager where I attended college, I unthinkingly replied, "MIT." He was obviously impressed and thankfully didn't ask anything more about it.

I started in the *Oregonian*'s circulation department, taking complaint calls from very angry people who hadn't received their morning newspaper, while continuing my journalism studies at Portland State College. At PSC (now Portland State University) I received the best writing instruction I have ever had. It came mainly from a highly experienced former newspaper reporter and editor, Wilma Morrison. She was likeable yet stern, a wisecracking heavy smoker who suffered no weak leads and—best for me, given my previous student persona—no classroom BS. Under Wilma's tutelage and her unrelenting insistence on clear, precise prose, I joined the staff of the Portland State student paper, the *Vanguard*, ultimately becoming its sports editor and weekly columnist—which, to my delight, paid for my tuition, $110 a term.

Afternoons I would walk the few blocks from Portland State's downtown campus to the Oregonian building on Broadway and my part-time job. Just walking into the paper made me dream of the future, and I soon left behind the circulation department and its irate callers to take a better-paying job in the newspaper's cashier's cage. There, my work didn't involve any cash at all but sending out the building's mail and, once a month, several hundred thousand bills to subscribers. It was boring and monotonous, but I was now convinced I'd be a reporter some day, and it thrilled me just to see the real reporters' names on mail coming in and going out.

My next part-time job at the paper was in the mailroom, where there isn't "mail" as you and I might know it. The mailroom is where newspapers are bundled before they're loaded into trucks and sent from the building; it's also where mailers, craft tradesmen, run large carousel-type machines that insert the funny pages, advertising tabs, and weekend feature magazines into the main body of the oversized Sunday newspaper. This is the primary work that goes on all week, interrupted regularly when alarms go off signaling that it's time to get out another edition of the paper. The mailers leave the inserter carousels and rush to the stacking and wire-tying machines to get the papers bundled and on their way to the street racks and subscribers' homes. (I think this noisy, dirty department got its name because it's where the papers of rural subscribers, after being wrapped in brown paper and given the proper postage, were sent out in mailbags.)

In the mailroom, I worked mostly with guys from Oklahoma— originally strikebreakers who came to Portland during a newspaper strike in the 1960s. They openly referred to themselves as "Okies" and treated part-time college kids like know-nothing, sorry sombitches, which is what they called us. As in, "Bring me that f———g spool of whar (wire), you sorry sombitch."

But they were otherwise good guys, and I learned a lot about work and life just listening to them talk—usually about where you could get the best deals on cars, and the latest tricks they'd used to cajole sex from their wives. I also learned that this was one newspaper department I didn't care to work in for long, but it was one floor closer to the editorial and sports departments, my hoped-for destinations.

When talking about my *Oregonian* experiences to others over the years, friends have wondered, especially since I was also writing for my college newspaper, why I didn't get a part-time, entry-level job writing for the daily paper. The truth is I did receive occasional inquiries from Portland's afternoon daily, the *Oregon Journal*, owned by the same company as the *Oregonian*. George Pasero, the well-known, longtime local sports editor, had even lifted portions of my columns in the *Vanguard* for attributed use in his own column, and would call me from time to time with an offer.

"You interested in a part-time job taking scores and doing high school stuff?" he'd say in his gruff, terse way. My heart would leap at the possibility, but the money being offered was always about $3 less an hour than I was making in the mailroom, and I'd have to decline.

"I don't think you're serious about being a sportswriter," Mr. Pasero would say before slamming down the phone, and I'd walk dejectedly back to the inserter machine to load up more *Parade* magazines. My secret plan was that I'd one day write a column so good that Mr. Pasero couldn't ignore me any longer and would have to call to offer me a full-time sportswriting job. Forget the scores and high school stories; I'd become the amazing young phenom on his staff, turning out creative, attention-getting copy every day for the *Journal* sports section.

However, that dream died a sudden death even before I left the mailroom. Company policy in those days required the personnel director to conduct annual interviews with employees—or maybe this was just for the part-time college guys, I've never been sure—to measure their future career plans.

The personnel director, Frank LeSage, was a natty executive in coat and tie, who wore horn-rimmed glasses and smoked a long, straight pipe, which sloped down ever so slightly toward the end. He reminded me of one of those middle-aged suburbanites that one of my favorite *MAD Magazine* artists was always drawing in his comic strips.

"What are your future goals?" Mr. LeSage asked kindly, taking a slight pull on his pipe—everybody smoked back then, even in their offices.

"I want to be a sportswriter," I said without hesitation, happy to finally share the plan with someone who might actually be in a position to do something about it.

"Good, good," he mused, while studying my resume. "How's your memory? A good sportswriter has to have a very good memory—you know, scores, dates, and such."

My heart fell. My memory was terrible, or more accurately, lazy, as the experts say. I had trouble recalling what I had for breakfast that day, let alone who had won the World Series only a few weeks before. I responded honestly, that my memory was awful. Mr. LeSage suggested that I might want to think about other jobs at the newspaper. "You could do a lot worse than being a mailer," he puffed, "it's good money and all."

That's pretty much all I remember about the interview with Mr. LeSage. When I left the *Oregonian* building that evening, stepping out onto Broadway into the chilling autumn air, it was like my dream had been taken from me, and I now believed I'd never be a sportswriter. I was one sorry sombitch.

CHAPTER THREE

Meanwhile, Back at the Whale...

*Broadcasting is really too important
to be left to the broadcasters.*
— *Tony Benn*

WHEN DOUG AND I finally hiked down the backside of the dune and reached the beach, we stopped briefly and placed on the sand what seemed like a ton of gear. The State Highway Department workers were still busy around the whale, and it didn't appear that an explosion would be happening anytime soon. No one was moving too fast.

One of the things I've never liked about being a television news reporter, versus a newspaper guy, is that you have to help lug a lot of crap everywhere you go. I'm sure Peter Jennings and Tom Brokaw don't do it anymore, if they ever did, but all reporters and anchor people at the local level are obliged to help schlep the tools of their trade. If you don't pack your fair share, and to those with "star" complexes this may mean nothing more than a microphone and a microphone cord, you're immediately labeled a prima donna by photographers who will forever avoid being assigned with you.

To capture our dead whale disposal story, we carried two cameras—Doug, a large Auricon sound film camera; me, a smaller Bolex silent film camera. We also had a cumbersome, heavy, wooden-legged tripod, and what we called the ditty bag, which contained extra film, various cords, batteries, microphones, gaffer's tape, and camera repair tools. At least we didn't have to pack lights for this job, since there was plenty of daylight, but as we took a short break to discuss just how we would go about covering the story, I looked at all of our stuff and mulled how easy print reporters had it. All they needed was a pen and pad—often they didn't even require a photographer to do a good job of reporting. But for any story with a strong visual element, as we thought an exploding whale certainly should have, the newspapers couldn't touch TV, which, in a way, made carrying all of the gear worth it.

Working together, Doug and I had developed a good relationship and understood the division of labor when it came to covering a story. He tried to get every shot that might possibly be needed, and I'd suggest shots he might miss and gather all necessary information. I would also line up and conduct any interviews that were needed. But many times, even while at a story, we were shooting in the dark, not really knowing what the story or its elements were. It was simply a matter of trying to capture all of the elements while simultaneously figuring out what the story *was*.

It helped that we had both started at Channel 2 doing the same entry-level job, editing news film. Doug had gone from being a film editor to the shooter's side of the business; I took the reporter's route. And for me, to be completely truthful, there was something else, besides a bad memory and a high school English teacher, which ultimately got me into broadcast journalism—my mom.

"You're so full of BS all of the time," she said to me one day shortly after my dream of newspaper sports writing had been crushed. "I think you ought to try taking some of that hot air into television." Mom may have had a rough way of saying things, but it turned out she was right.

I knocked on the doors of Portland's local television stations, and the news director at one of them, KATU, told me he'd consider me for the night film editor's job if the position ever became vacant—*and* if I came in on my own time and learned how to do it. I did, and when the film editor who taught me quit shortly thereafter, I became film editor of KATU's eleven o'clock newscast. In retrospect, there couldn't have been a better position for learning the business of television news.

I worked nightly with reporters' scripts, matching photographers' pictures with the writers' words, trying mightily to make sure the film we put on the air told the same story as the written narration, which isn't always the case, as any regular news viewer knows. (How disconcerting can it be when the anchorperson reports, "Police say the suspect entered this house," and the shot isn't a house at all, but a car or a bystander? Some editor isn't paying attention, and the writer hasn't checked the video against the script.)

I learned to enjoy the physical act of actually cutting and gluing the film together with a hot splicer—it seemed to meet some previously undiscovered need for doing something creative with hands and mind. I also liked running the film through my viewer to find the right scenes, then placing them in the proper order to carry a story visually. I learned very quickly that even a part-time film editor wields major power; I could make, say, an antiwar demonstration look like either a hellish riot or a sleepy nonevent, based on the scenes I chose to use.

I could also make the newsroom phones ring off the hook if some demonstrator burned an American flag, and I chose to put it in the story. For me, it raised a question every time—do I use the burning flag or not? An angry horde burning a flag, versus a few protesters torching one in relative quiet, could have the same emotional impact on viewers, but was the use of such scenes warranted? Did they tell the real story of what took place? All of this gave me an instant respect for the power of television, and a lifelong commitment to getting things right, no matter my own bias or point of view. It also helped me to understand how the marriage of words and pictures works, and as a result, I don't believe that as a reporter I have ever asked a photographer or editor to do something with film or video that couldn't technically be done. Not many television reporters and writers I know can make that boast—even though our medium is, bottom line, mostly about pictures. Some never understand that.

I was going to class at Portland State in the mornings, working on my sports section and column for the college paper in the afternoons, and spending my nights in the Channel 2 newsroom. I found myself giving the greatest amount of energy and attention to the television work and the least amount to my studies. My coworkers in the newsroom had also begun letting me write scripts, which were actually used in the late evening newscasts, and that was an education in itself.

The first time I heard a newscaster read on the air something I had written, I couldn't believe it. It didn't matter that before beginning my now nightly writing chores, I'd had to retrieve old scripts from the trash to study their format—literally to see how the words were supposed to look on the page. But since my scripts were used on the air, I figured that must make me a professional writer. Nearly as quickly as my sportswriter dreams had died, the possibility of a new career suddenly loomed before me: TV reporter! And it would become reality faster than I could ever imagine.

Newsrooms forever seem to be short of writers, and it wasn't long before my boss, a likeable news director (words which are rarely if ever used together anymore!) named Dick Hawkins, asked if I could do some part-time writing on our weekend newscasts. Shortly after that, when we were short on reporters, I started going out on stories. My very first television interview was with a personal, political hero, Senator Wayne Morse, the renowned "Tiger of the Senate," one of only two senators who voted against the Gulf of Tonkin Resolution that authorized the use of American military forces in Vietnam. I can still remember how badly my knees and hands were shaking as I interviewed Senator Morse, but I have no recollection whatsoever of what I may have interviewed him about.

And before I knew it, I was actually appearing on television as well. Mr. Hawkins told me to do a "stand-up" for one of my weekend stories—that's where the reporter is seen standing on location somewhere and talking into the camera. The first time I ever appeared on Portland television news, it was for a feature report on a local facility for young, unwed mothers, the Salvation Army's White Shield Home.

Don't ever let anyone tell you that there isn't a lot of ego gratification involved in working in television. I don't know if my story on the home for young mothers was any good, but I sure liked seeing myself on TV! More importantly, I also felt I was contributing to the public good by telling our audience about the work being done at the Home—who knew?

Without anyone instructing me much in how to do it, I seemed to be becoming a professional news reporter, and it had a pretty good feel to it. Maybe my future was in broadcast, not print.

———

Doug became a news photographer in much the same way that I became a reporter, primarily by doing it. We were assigned to cover a number of stories together, and quickly discovered that we had quite an edge over the other two-person teams in our news department.

Because both of us could edit film, and most reporters couldn't, we could get a breaking news story on the air faster than the others. Returning from, say, a fatal car wreck, I'd write the script while Doug took the raw film upstairs for processing. By the time it was developed (or out of the soup, as the old-timers liked to say), my narration was complete and Doug began editing the silent film, or B-roll. If we'd interviewed someone, an eyewitness or a cop, I'd take the sound film and pull the appropriate sound bites, rushing that film over to Doug to be edited into the main story in the places called for by my script. This system completely eliminated the need for the reporter to stand next to the editor, directing him back and forth through the film, to find the sound portions. If the story was particularly long or more complex, I could also help Doug edit the B-roll.

We soon became the team du jour for breaking news, and since we spent a great deal of time chasing cops and firefighters, we took to privately calling ourselves the "video death rangers." It was pure fun for a couple of young guys, and the excitement just kept coming, day after day, even in little old Portland, Oregon.

———

This exploding whale thing, though, had us wondering. What was the real story here, and what did we have to do to get it? Who were the principals, the talking heads, and what questions would we want to ask someone about to put a stick of dynamite up a dead whale's backside, or wherever they were going to put it? I mean, was blasting whales routine for state highway workers, or was this some experiment to see if it would actually work as a method of disposal? If the latter were true, they might not be thrilled that a TV news team from Portland had arrived on the beach with their cameras.

"I guess I'll just go and start shooting this thing," Doug said as he started to gather up the gear.

"I'll find someone who knows what's going on," I responded, picking up my own load. Doug took the silent camera (which in those days was used to shoot the B-roll, because silent film was cheaper than sound film); I looked for a safe spot to temporarily stow the sound camera.

"But just do me one favor, Doug," I added. "Let's not somehow miss this thing. If they blow up a whale and we don't get it on film, coming all this way and all, we're screwed."

"What? They're going to blow up a whale?" Doug asked in mock horror. And he trudged off through the dry sand toward the carcass.

CHAPTER FOUR

Video Death Rangers

For the *New York Times*, it's "all the news that's fit to print."
For a television newscast, it's all the news that fits.
—Anonymous

THE LATE SIXTIES, 1968 to be precise, was a great time to begin a career as a news reporter. Oh, there wasn't that much going on in Portland, because there never is—a local historian would later comment about this period that the buildings you saw in the city in 1962 were pretty much the same buildings that were there in 1932— but there was plenty happening nationally and internationally, with local implications.

American combat troops arrived in Vietnam in 1962, and the entire country was involved in a clamorous debate about whether the United States should be there at all. About 57,000 Oregonians would serve in Southeast Asia; 800 of them—many of them friends and former class-mates—would die or be listed as missing in action. There were daily antiwar protests and demonstrations in nearly all cities across the country, Portland included.

In retrospect, if I was at all serious about a career in journalism, I should have tried to get to Vietnam as a war correspondent. Covering wars was how many of the great reporters got their start, Edward R. Murrow and his cronies having taken this route by reporting on World War II in Europe. But I never considered doing the same by going to Southeast Asia; trying to cover a story while someone in black pajamas shot at you didn't sound at all appealing. Instead, I did everything possible to avoid the draft and keep my student deferment—well, everything but maintaining the required college GPA, which ultimately landed me in an Oregon Army National Guard unit.

I also got married in 1968, and soon Vicki and I were expecting our first child.

It was a good time to stay right where I was and learn how to become a television news reporter. Since I was also still a full-time student, I had to juggle news assignments with my class schedule. It somehow worked, and Channel 2 seemed to be continually in need of someone to cover something. It could be confusing playing both roles, though. I can recall participating in a student antiwar protest on the PSC campus in the morning, and then covering another downtown student protest as a reporter in the afternoon. I eventually decided I couldn't ethically do both, and stopped involving myself in events that might somehow impact my neutrality as a reporter.

My boss at the time was a terse, no-nonsense guy named Bruce Baer. Bruce had become quite well known in Portland as a political reporter before becoming our assignment editor.

"Just go out and get the story, sweetie pie," Bruce would bark at me if I'd ask too many questions about whatever he had assigned me. And fortunately, because he knew I enjoyed politics, Bruce had me spend at least a week covering each of the presidential candidates who visited the Northwest during the crowded 1968 campaign.

It was exciting for a twenty-one-year-old to meet such men of achievement, hanging out with the likes of Nelson Rockefeller, Eugene McCarthy, Hubert Humphrey, George McGovern, Richard Nixon, and others, asking them questions and trying to put them on the spot.

It was also an education in how a reporter must deal with his own personal bias and prejudices. Politically, I favored the Democrat Robert F. Kennedy, whose campaign I spent several days covering during the Oregon primary, only weeks before he was assassinated in Los Angeles in June. I loathed the independent candidate, erstwhile Alabama governor George Wallace, a former segregationist who had done all he could to block the civil rights movement in the South. But when I met and interviewed both, I found Kennedy somewhat aloof and distant, while Wallace was all charm and warmth. If I were to go back into the film files today and look again at stories I'd done on their respective campaign swings through Oregon, I'd likely discover that I did a better job of reporting on Wallace than on Kennedy, an overreaction to dealing with my own prejudice. Plus, Wallace had done the better job of trying to win me over.

The hardest part of that political year was being the lead reporter on the campaign of a former Oregon state legislator, Bob Packwood, who was attempting the impossible in trying to unseat my hero, Senator Wayne Morse. I saw how easy it could be for a reporter, in vying with other reporters for airtime and preferred story position, to become an advocate for the candidate he was covering, and so it was all the harder to take when Packwood successfully ended Senator Morse's twenty-four-year Senate reign. I felt somehow responsible.

I also felt the education I was receiving while covering politics and general news was better than anything I was learning in the classroom at Portland State, and some of my more enlightened instructors seemed to agree. One of them, a political science professor named Burton Onstine, approved of my suggestion that I produce a "blooper" film on the candidates' visits to Oregon in lieu of a term paper on the primary election, which the rest of the class was assigned. There were plenty of outtakes from the station's political coverage, which were never used on the air. Back then, we weren't in the practice of making candidates look like stumblebums, at least not until Gerald Ford came along.

It was easy to edit together a large reel of hilarious gaffes and malapropisms from the candidates, with Richard Milhous Nixon, a man who could misspeak himself in the most humorous ways, being the primary player. My classmates loved it, and it earned me an A, one of my last college grades. I'd leave school shortly thereafter to become a full-time television news reporter.

At Channel 2 I found myself working regularly with about a half-dozen photographers, all of them good guys and most with years of experience. My preference, though, was to work with the other new guy, Doug Brazil. He and I kind of figured out what we were supposed to do as we went, laughing our way through many an embarrassing situation as two neophytes trying to pass themselves off as seasoned news professionals.

It seemed we were always forgetting an essential piece of equipment, like a camera; and we loved the way some national figure, like the vice president of the United States, would size us up as we set up for an interview. It was as if they assumed we were a couple of gofers who set the lights and got the camera ready for the real news team, but then we'd sit down and do the interview. "Are we starting now?" I remember Senator George McGovern asking incredulously after I'd already begun my questioning.

Doug and I were capable of making our own fun while on assignment, too. We thought it only appropriate to hit the local tavern to celebrate with the old VFW guys we'd just covered in Albany's big Veterans' Day parade. I also remember once, after covering author Ken Kesey's impassioned yet confusing speech in support of a marijuana legalization measure, trying to sort out what he'd actually said over a few beers. Just about everyone drank at lunch in those days, but Doug and I probably overdid it a little on that occasion. Returning to the newsroom, I tried to write the story, putting together a couple of graphs (as journalists call paragraphs) on Kesey, basically about who he was and where he spoke. I then told Doug to choose a couple of sound bites himself; it didn't really matter what he had Kesey saying, I explained, since nothing he said made sense anyway.

With that, we filed what had to be one of the lamest stories in the history of television news in Portland, but our five o'clock anchors presented it with appropriate authority, as if whatever Ken Kesey said was newsworthy. No one working on the newscast, not the producer or the anchors, asked us for an explanation for such a sorry piece of work—until the next day.

"That story you guys did on Kesey and the marijuana referendum?" the newsroom secretary inquired as I passed her desk. "Was it me or did that make no sense whatsoever?" It didn't, but no one else seemed to notice, least of all the viewers.

We also distinguished ourselves one spring by volunteering to cover the selection of each of the Portland Rose Festival's thirteen high school princesses, a much-dreaded but required annual news ritual in our town. Our offer came with the condition that we not be assigned a single other Rose Festival event for the summer, and there were scores of them.

I prepared a script template and simply filled in the blanks each day, leaving time for the requisite screaming by students at the selection ceremonies, and such enlightened fill-in-the-blanks information, as: "_Julie_, the daughter of Mr. and Mrs. _Howard Adams_, plans to attend _The University of Oregon_ to study _communications_, and hopes to be _a newscaster_ someday."

The anchors did complain that time that I was turning in the same script every day, but Bruce Baer, who also produced our five o'clock news, defended it. "It *is* the same story every day," he answered, happy not to have to find a different crew to cover the dreaded princess selections every day for two weeks.

But our greatest claim to fame in those early years of working together was a spoof story inspired by something I'd seen from the BBC, the British Broadcasting Corporation. Some fun-loving reporter had done a completely bogus story on the "spaghetti harvest" in Italy, actually showing workers on ladders removing what appeared to be cooked strands of pasta from trees. It was hilarious, and Doug and I decided to see how American audiences, or at least the one in Portland, would take to a total spoof.

We chose as our subject a two-headed dog, which in reality happened to be my wife's two Maltese puppies. Using a camera trick or two, we made it appear that the dog had a head on each end of his body, and we put our story on the air on April Fool's Day, with just a slight hint from the anchor, who introduced the story by advising viewers they could believe it or not.

No story in the television station's history brought the response that one did, with our telephones ringing for days, people wanting to see the story, and the dog, again.

The president of the local animal defenders league chapter called to demand that the dog be put to sleep (we had reported that one of the dog's problems was that he often tried to walk in opposite directions at once, causing a great strain on the middle part of his body).

The vice president and general manager of Channel 2—my big boss—called me to his office to ask if I could arrange a weekend visit with the dog for him and his grandchildren. This presented another journalistic problem for a rookie reporter: How do you tell your boss he has been completely sucked in by a phony story that appeared on his own TV station's newscast?

Our reputation as the "we'll cover anything once" guys (and, if they're Rose Princesses, thirteen times) continued to grow, along with our ability to get breaking news on the air, fast.

Doug and I concluded years later that when it was discovered that some state workers were preparing to dynamite a whale, we were the only team that could have been selected for the job.

CHAPTER FIVE

Pregnant Olympians
and Prison Riots

But if it pleases you to hear the news of the world,
you must always suffer disquiet of heart as a result.
—*Thomas á Kempis,* The Imitation of Christ, *1418*

I REALLY WANTED to get a good, close look at the whale. Or rather, I
did and I didn't. It's like when you're driving down the road and see a
dead animal of some kind on the shoulder, you want to see what it is,
but you don't want to look. Not many of us get to walk right up to a
whale and look him right in the eye (if, in fact, this whale was a "him").
And would its eye be open or shut?

Potential writing problems had also started coming to mind. If
simple sentences about looking at a whale, or how it looked back,
seemed troublesome, how would I accurately and concisely report on
one getting blown up? The writing process, I was learning, actually
starts while the reporter is still in the field collecting information. And
no matter the subject, the question at the heart of the job is always the
same: Can I explain this?

I'd also need a good look at the whale, which had died of
unknown causes, for personal storytelling purposes. The experienced
reporters in our newsroom always came back from an assignment with
great inside accounts of the story behind the story—anecdotes
invariably more interesting or funny than what they put on the air.

Some would be told for years, shared with luncheon and banquet audiences if good enough, and every reporter seemed to have a few favorites, which were recalled over drinks after work, on the golf course, on fishing trips.

As I walked through the sand in the general direction of the big, stinky mammal, I pondered why these "inside" stories were never shared with the viewers, as they might make for much better newscasts. Whatever the case, I knew I must force myself to get a good look at my decaying subject or I wouldn't have much to tell to anyone.

I could see that Doug was also moving closer to the carcass, shooting as he went. There was a commonly accepted method of filming a story in those days, having to do with getting the requisite number of wide, or establishing shots; cutaways, such as people's faces, to be used mainly as bridges between the other scenes in editing; medium shots; tight shots; and so on.

In the years since, most television photographers have gone a different way, ignoring the establishing shots (geez, if we shot a story in a building, we invariably shot an "establisher" of the outside of the place), which really set the scene and give a story its visual context. It's why, when watching the news with friends or in some public place, I invariably hear someone ask, "What's that?" as they try to comprehend what they are seeing on the film or video. The pictures are not there, or haven't been built in proper order to establish the scene and to create the necessary visual understanding. Doug Brazil was very, very good at doing it right.

As I moved steadily toward the whale, I looked around and made some observations. A reporter likes to appear is if he or she knows what's going on, so I tried to act nonchalant, like I had attended several mammal bombings. There were a couple of dozen people on the beach in the immediate area, but there didn't seem to be other television news crews present; at least, I couldn't see anyone else with professional film cameras or tripods. There might be a stringer or two around—freelance photographers hired by the other Portland stations—but I couldn't be sure.

This was good—mine might be the only in-depth television story. My practice whenever I covered a story that the other stations were on was to rush immediately to a TV set after finishing my work to see how the competition did it. Apparently lacking in self-assurance, I sought confirmation that I had found the right "hook" and gotten my facts correct. If there were no other TV reporters on the beach, I wouldn't have to later measure my story against others. (I eventually quit this practice after hearing a reporter for Portland's CBS affiliate state in a story that spring flooding on the North Coast was so bad, and the water so high in places, that it "reached the uteruses" of cows grazing in the fields. I may be a city guy, but I was fairly certain that the word he meant to use was "udders," and after that I no longer felt compelled to monitor the competition.)

Not far across the beach, I saw a man wearing a silver hard hat, standing about fifty feet from the carcass, talking to a couple of guys who may have been print reporters. One of them was wearing a suit and seemed to be taking notes. The hard-hat might be the expert I needed to talk to, and I'd make my way over to him as soon as I got a good look at the deceased. One thing I needed to determine was just how close I could get—was my access limited or any way restricted by whoever was in charge of the job? This was, after all, a blast site, and I had previously learned, the hard way, never to go where I wasn't permitted, news reporter or not.

───────

It happened in 1968, just after I'd begun writing for our weekend news shows, and proved to be the major break that elevated me immediately to the position of full-time news reporter.

I was in the newsroom late on a Saturday afternoon, our five o'clock program had already begun, and I was about to take another look at what was coming over the incessantly clattering Associated Press and United Press International teletype machines. It was part of my job to make sure we weren't missing any breaking news stories, which would be an especially unprofessional thing to do when your news program was actually on the air.

I'd come to love the teletypes, or the wires as we called them. Imagine—in the days prior to the Internet, twenty-four-hour cable news networks, and all-news radio—being able to stand at a machine and read stories from all over the world, being written, or at least typed, at that very moment by who knows whom, who knows where. International news, sports, local news, farm reports, weather, you name it, was constantly being delivered to the closet-sized, not-so-soundproof room that housed our wire machines. I could stand there and read what was happening before anyone else knew it, and I enjoyed doing so for long periods of time. With that came the obligation to "tear" the wires, ripping off the individual stories and filing them by category and subject; otherwise, the long sheets of paper would back up behind the machines, eventually clogging the teletype so badly it could no longer print.

Because practical jokes were more common in newsrooms in those days, I'd also discovered how to have a little fun with the machines. I'd take blank wire paper—AP's was always yellow, UPI's always white—and having found a newsroom typewriter whose typeface matched that of the teletypes, I'd compose phony wire stories. I'd then rush them into the studio, hand them to the news anchorman during a commercial break, and see if I could fool him into using one on the air.

One such prank took place during an eleven o'clock newscast. The Winter Olympic Games were taking place in Grenoble, France, and there had been some question whether or not a skier from the Northwest named Kiki Cutter would have to return home without competing due to illness. The story I composed had her coming home, not because of sickness, but because she had become pregnant by a famous French skier, Jean-Claude Killy.

I wrote it as a "BULLETIN"—the word in caps at the top of the page and the story double-spaced, as bulletins always were—and ran it into the studio. I purposely waited until the last few seconds of the commercial break to hand it to an anchorman named Bill Bartholomew, so he wouldn't have a chance to read it in advance. "Use this right away," I hurriedly advised him, "it's big!"

Bill, who'd become a good friend and my main writing mentor on the night shift, went back on the air and at once used the phrase so common in the early days of TV news. "This just handed me," he intoned seriously. But even as he said it, he took my fake story from his left hand, glanced at it, and passed it to his right, setting it on the desk and out of camera view.

"Now to other news," Bill went on without missing a beat, much to my disappointment. My little joke had been discovered—this guy was too good!

He was laughing hard when he returned to the newsroom after the show.

"Man, you almost got me," he howled. "If the word 'pregnant' hadn't jumped out at me, I would have read it for sure." We had a good time talking about the prospect of his doing so, but I can't recall it being mentioned that both of us would have likely lost our jobs had Bill actually reported my "news." It was a different time, and having fun was always acceptable in the newsroom, even if it often crossed the lines of good taste and, at times, put careers in jeopardy. I wouldn't say that "having fun" is very acceptable in today's newsroom, and that's sad. For people who deal daily with the world at its worst, comic relief is good and necessary therapy.

On that Saturday in 1968, the teletypes' bells began ringing, which signaled that a bulletin was coming across. I ran to the wire room and read the story as it moved—inmates at the Oregon State Penitentiary in Salem, the state's capital, were rioting. They had set fire to a part of the prison, taken over another section, and had taken guards as hostages. I waited for the bulletin to reach a paragraph break, tore it from the machine, and raced it to the news studio.

"This one's for real," I advised the anchor, perhaps fearing my practical jokes might catch up with me, and he read the story cold on the air. During the next commercial break, the anchor directed me to run back to the newsroom and get the boss on the phone, he would tell me what to do next.

I called the news director, Dick Hawkins, who said I should call a reporter and photographer at home and get them moving immediately to Salem, that I should just go down the names on the newsroom roster until I found two who could go. It might be difficult to find anyone on a Saturday evening, but I got on the phone. It seemed logical to call the chief photographer first, so I tried Carl Vermilya, a veteran shooter who had come to television after years of taking still photos for the *Oregonian*. (Nearly all photographers in the early days of TV news came from newspapers; nearly all of the reporters came from radio.)

"I'll be at the station in fifteen minutes," Carl told me, "have a reporter meet me there."

I tried the first reporter on the list—no answer. It was the same with the second; the third's line was busy. I began to worry. Carl would arrive at the station soon, and I didn't have a reporter for him. Then it hit me—*I* was a reporter. Maybe I was only a weekend part-timer, but I had covered breaking news stories before and couldn't think of a reason why I couldn't cover this one.

I called Mr. Hawkins back, telling him I had a photographer on the way, but, uh, couldn't seem to get in touch with a reporter. "You go," he said without hesitation.

The ride to Salem, normally forty-five minutes to an hour from Northeast Portland, went by in a blur. We used flashy, Ford Mustang fastbacks as news cars in those days, and Carl, one of the older guys on our staff, drove with the expertise of someone well used to getting places fast. Nearing the exit for the penitentiary, I glanced toward the prison—still two or three miles to the west but visible from the freeway—and could see flames shooting high in the sky. This thing was for real, and my heart raced at the prospect of seeing what a real-life prison riot might be like. Oddly, I felt no fear or nervousness over what might be expected of me as a reporter.

We quickly parked the car, gathered up our gear, and ran in the direction of the nearest activity. A Salem Fire Department hook-and-ladder truck was parked near the administration building, its longest ladder extended over the prison wall. Firemen and guards were bringing people who appeared to be inmates, wearing blue denim pants and shirts, down the ladder. Maybe these were the ringleaders, and the riot would soon be over. Carl and I hurried over to film what was happening, Carl shooting his silent film camera, me operating a portable, battery-operated light, another of the reporter's duties during all nighttime shoots in those days.

Almost as soon as we were set and rolling film, Carl and I were simultaneously struck in the back with some kind of hard object, not with enough force to be injured or knocked to the ground, but certainly enough to get our attention and to stop Carl's filming. We turned to see that two prison guards had poked us pretty good with what appeared to be white ax handles.

"You can't be in this area," one of them shouted, "please go back to the parking area immediately."

We did as we were told, joining a group of other newspeople who were shooting from a distance the same activity Carl and I had just charged into. Apparently, just before we arrived, prison officials had set up a line of demarcation for the gathering press, indicating that no one should come closer than the parking lot to get their pictures of what was going on. We also learned that the prisoners being brought over the wall were not involved in the riot at all, but were in an education class in the administration building and were being removed so that the rioters couldn't enlist them or, in the alternative, take them hostage.

Thus began a long night. Around one or two o'clock in the morning, the riot's ringleaders insisted on meeting with the prison administration and the governor's representatives to air their grievances. One of their demands, backed up by the rioters' sending out a badly beaten guard every hour or so, was that the press be present at the negotiations. And so a group of us were led through several barred doors, which clanked shut behind us, deep into the bowels of the smoke-filled administration building, to a windowless room where the two sides would meet face-to-face.

Carl and I barely had time to find a spot to set up our sound camera when a prison official asked for everyone's attention. The inmates—an awful-looking group of toughs, who were far more terrifying than anyone you would see in a prison movie—had sat down at one table, the state officials at another facing them.

The official spoke loudly and urgently when the room didn't quiet quickly enough.

"Listen up, everybody," he said. "I know everyone in this room has been in dangerous situations before and there won't be any panic, but I've just been told that the two floors above us are on fire. We're supposed to sit tight and let the firefighters do their jobs—we'll be okay."

No, I thought, I am going to panic. This was bad, and all I could think about was that series of barred doors which had locked tight behind us as we descended into this death trap. What had I done to deserve dying in a prison? But before I could seriously consider my chances of making a break for the outside, it was announced that the fire had been put out above, that we could actually stay where we were and the negotiations could begin.

They went on all night. The inmates were unbelievably profane and disrespectful of the officials and governor's people—"you mutha-f————s have no f———— idea what really goes on in this f————s—hole," a convicted murdered named Bowles shouted at the governor's men; but the prison officials were just as indignant toward the riot leaders—at one point the top corrections guy yelled back at the baddest looking dude in the room, "We don't have to take this kind of crap from the likes of vermin like you."

All of this, of course, to a twenty-one-year-old news reporter, was incredible, real-life drama, and I'd force myself to duck out of the negotiations every couple of hours or so to send an updated report back to the station. Another photographer showed up the next morning to relieve Carl, but I didn't take so much as a break until early Sunday afternoon, the talks still in progress, when a Channel 2 reporter named Dean Jones arrived and told me the boss wanted me back at the station right away.

"How come I haven't had a replacement yet?" I asked Dean, "they've sent two new photographers but you're the first reporter I've seen."

"You don't get it, do you?" he said. "Every reporter back there is yelling and screaming to get down here, but Hawkins said it was your story, and he held them all back."

It was quite a contrast to the way things are done today in television news, with highly touted "team coverage," and two or three reporters assigned various aspects of the same story, which frequently in our case is a big storm that often fails to materialize. (And, oh yes, we like to put names on such coverage, like "The Winter Storm Team." I wonder if such things impress our viewers or help drive them away.)

I jumped into the Mustang that Dean had driven to Salem and headed back to town, happy to be out of the prison, and happier still to be tooling a marked television news car up the freeway. I'd never driven one before, and secretly hoped other motorists would be looking into the car to see which of their news heroes was at the wheel. It even made me forget about the prison riot and my fatigue for a while.

Upon my return, Dick Hawkins and I wrote and produced a half-hour special on the prison riot, which aired that evening even while the riot was still going on. This was also unheard of at the time, which may surprise viewers familiar with all of the breaking news we constantly cover today. Back then, everything was captured on film and stories usually aired considerably after a news event had run its course, perhaps in the next scheduled newscast. Producing a prison-riot special with the riot still in progress was a most uncommon occurrence, unlike today when TV can "go live" with any news event at any time and stay with it as long as necessary.

I arrived home that evening just in time to watch our little special with my wife, Vicki, but I fell asleep on the floor long before it ended, my nonstop weekend of work finally catching up with me.

"Look, look," Vicki shouted, picking my head up from the floor and pointing it toward the TV set. The program was over and credits were rolling on the screen; the one that had gotten Vicki's attention read, "Co-Producer—Paul Linnman."

Like I say, I was a news reporter from that day forward, no more part-time writing and film editing for me.

And never again would I walk into any breaking news situation without first making darn sure where I was and was not allowed to go. You only have to meet up with a prison guard's ax handle once to learn the lesson.

I had now almost reached the whale and could see that the people closest to it were transportation department workers and also, to my surprise, your basic bystanders. There were beachcombers and passersby, plus some who had obviously come out expressly to see the whale. If these people had access, even as the workers were getting ready to explode the thing, no one was likely to stop me.

In such close proximity, the stench was overpowering. However, the whale, said to be a Pacific gray, really wasn't that much to look at. It was about shoulder high, its tail fin flat on the sand, with its huge torso turning slightly, so that it was all but lying on its side. It was black and shades of gray, with some flesh-colored patches near what I took to be its mouth, though both the mouth and eyes, which were shut, were hard to make out. It's skin seemed old and weathered.

I guess it looked just about how you might imagine a dead whale laying on the beach to look, as unremarkable and nondescript as the countless oversized rocks found all along the Oregon coast. Except this one stunk, bad.

The worker on the small bulldozer was now making his way to near where I was standing. His front loader was filled with cardboard boxes, and as he drew closer, I could make out the words "Dangerous" and "High Explosives" written in yellow and red on the tops of the boxes. I also saw a man walking in my direction wearing dark coveralls and carrying a little box with a plunger and wires coming out of the top— a detonator, just like the ones used by cartoon characters Wile E. Coyote and Daffy Duck. It embarrassed me to realize these things weren't the creation of animators; in reality, someone would soon give that little plunger a push and cause a blast of such magnitude that it would dispose of an eight-ton whale.

I looked around for the guy with the silver hard hat, who was now standing toward the front of the whale and taking a Polaroid picture of it. I needed to go talk to him, and to get away from the unbelievable smell—and all of that dynamite.

CHAPTER SIX

And Now Some Other Amavng Mammals

And Now Some Other
Amazing Mammals

**When people open their hearts to God and allow Him to be
their partner, and His genius to flow through them, the
most wonderful dreams become reality.**
—*Father Joe Girzone*, Joshua and the City, 1995

I ONLY LASTED FIVE YEARS as a hard news reporter. There were many
reasons why, but chief among them was the most common complaint
about television news, which I've also heard from viewers over the
years: it's all bad news.

It was exciting at first for a young reporter to follow presidential
candidates and to chase after cops and firefighters at crime scenes and
various disasters. However, for every Robert Kennedy I interviewed,
there was a grieving parent of a murdered gang member I was asked to
question.

There were also too many stories I loathed doing: financial or
economic pieces that didn't lend themselves to pictures; or animal
abuse cases, where the pictures were so bad you didn't want to look at
them, let alone put them on the air. Indeed, there were many more
interminably boring city council or board of higher education meetings
to cover than there were prison riots or, yes, whale bombings.

After a relatively short time, it starts to grind you down, especially
if you don't have a passion for serious news, as I found I didn't. And

since it's serious news that fills a newscast and there aren't many spots for feature reporters, I decided to leave television and take a job as an aide to a Portland City Council member, hoping local government would give me the opportunity to make some positive contributions to my community.

I was wrong. Nearly everything I worked on at city hall was also, in the main, bad news, some kind of unsolvable problem that invariably had citizens extremely upset with my boss or me. But these people weren't like angry viewers; they continually pointed out that their tax money paid my salary and they acted as if they owned me.

Five years of that and I went right back to television. This time, however, it was on the bright side of the business, on a features program called *Evening*, which was produced at Portland's NBC affiliate, KGW-TV. The show followed the evening news, and had been successful and innovative. I signed on as cohost, working nightly with a bright young woman named Robin Chapman, and along with the others on the program's very creative reporting staff, spent my days producing feature stories, or, good news.

Evening evolved into a like program called *PM Magazine*, the main difference being that the new show had access to syndicated features from the "PM" network and less innovation, but we still produced our own local feature stories, which I found I loved to do. In fact, that was the start of what I've done in all of the years since, telling stories of ordinary people who do extraordinary things.

Instead of the excitement of chasing news stories, feature reporting brought the pure joy of upbeat storytelling. It also allowed me to meet some incredible people—virtually anyone I wanted to, who was doing something of note.

Imagine hearing or reading about a person you found to be inspi-rational, say a physically-challenged athlete who overcomes her handicap to become a national champion, or a foster parent who is raising a house full of drug-affected children, and then getting to meet them. You're free to ask them anything—what drives them, why they do what they do, what the returns are—and then craft their responses into a story which may benefit countless others just by the telling.

I've reported on virtually thousands of such people in the past quarter century, and I've never run out of subjects. There always seems to be one more good person who has found creative and wonderful ways to give back or achieve personal goals, no matter how impossible those goals may seem at first.

And of all of these incredible subjects, I'd put one man's story at the top of the list as the most important I've ever covered.

———————

Ron Post, to me anyway, has never looked the various parts he's played. As a young man, he sang bass in two rock vocal groups of the 1960s, the Del Vikings and the La Chords. I just can't picture this straight-looking beanpole—a six-foot-five-inch white guy—gyrating around on stage with three African Americans as they performed their top-ten hit, "To Be Loved."

Ron is one of those men who looks like he was born in a business suit, a kindly, soft-spoken sort with glasses and mustache, someone who is quick to smile and then, as if embarrassed, just as quick to purse his lips and suppress the grin.

In no way does he look like someone who would set out to save the world. But that's what he did.

In 1979, Ron and his wife, Jean, were watching the evening news on television. Ron was a successful Salem businessman, a hardworking entrepreneur who had started or taken over a number of businesses. He knew how to take companies in trouble and turn them around. As the couple watched the news, they became deeply moved by disturbing footage of Cambodian refugees fleeing to Thailand to escape the cruel dictator Pol Pot and the "Killing Fields," a term made familiar in this century by the movie of that name. Tragically, the refugee camps in Thailand became full of Cambodians by the thousands who were sick and dying from a lack of food and medical care.

The Posts were greatly troubled by what they were watching. Ron gazed across the living room at his teenage daughter, Sheri, who was sleeping on the couch. He wondered why he and his family were blessed to be born in America and not in Cambodia, like the suffering parents and children he saw on the news.

"As I pondered that thought," Ron would later write, "a plan entered my mind as clearly as though someone had written it on paper and handed it to me. The plan was simple, but very precise: recruit a medical team and lead it to help the Cambodians in two weeks' time." He got up from his easy chair and went to work.

Of course such a plan seemed impossible, and Ron had no idea where to begin. He called the local newscaster he had seen reporting the Cambodia story, and after a brief conversation decided to hold a press conference in Portland to put out a call for volunteers. There was a major setback when two doctors he had invited to attend, both former missionaries, unexpectedly informed Ron in front of the assembled media that his idea wouldn't work, that it would take at least two months to assemble such a team, and that doctors and nurses could never leave their practices on such short notice.

Ron, a deeply religious man, felt momentarily defeated. "Lord," he prayed, "I really felt you wanted me to do this. Please Lord, help me!"

At that moment, Ron's personal physician, Dr. Van Volkinburg, whom he had invited to attend the press conference for moral support, spoke up to say that he could go on such a mission in two weeks, and immediately volunteered to do so.

That seemed to be all it took. After that evening's newscasts, the Post's telephone rang for two weeks as they heard from scores of people who wanted to volunteer, and not just medical types. An attorney called to say that he would come do anything—empty waste baskets in the temporary office Ron had set up, if nothing else; a real estate agent wanted to know what he could do; still others, many others, simply called to give money.

In two weeks' time, the Posts collected $250,000 in donations, selected a medical team of twenty-eight volunteers, and, impossibly, secured all of the volunteers' passports and visas. Because it was a grassroots effort and Ron wanted everyone in his home region to feel a part of it, he called the volunteer group the "Northwest Medical Teams."

Arriving in Thailand, the new volunteers were asked to run a 125-bed hospital ward and care for hundreds of outpatients, a task that seemed absolutely daunting. Now Ron was seeing great suffering face-to-face, not on his television screen, and with so many sick and dying around them, he feared that his volunteers would be overwhelmed by what was before them.

"But I underestimated the team," he said. "Each began helping one person at a time, and each would make a difference, one life at a time."

When the volunteers first went to work, local authorities told them that thirty to forty people died each day in their location, the Sa Keao Refugee Camp. During the two weeks the Northwest Medical Teams volunteers worked tirelessly in the field hospital they had been assigned, not one person died. They had made an impact, and Ron Post's plan—the one given him as if it had been written on paper—had worked.

————————

Ron returned to Salem to go back to work, only to find that he was unable to keep his mind on business.

"The fulfillment had been stripped away," he said. "Spending my time making money just didn't make sense. How could it when I had witnessed such tragic events and had played a part in changing them?"

Ron Post didn't know it at the time, but he was on the brink of spending the next twenty years of his life directing lifesaving help to millions of people in dozens of countries. The survivors of earthquakes in El Salvador and Armenia, the victims of famine in Ethiopia, the medically indigent of Mexico, even the homeless and migrant workers in his native state of Oregon, would all be touched by Ron and the Northwest Medical Teams he had begun.

By 1997, I had reported on the teams and Ron Post numerous times, and had helped host several live telethons to raise money for the organization. It seemed that all we had to do was put Ron on live television, let him talk from his heart for a few minutes about the hurting people of the world, and our phones would ring madly, affluent viewers calling to donate thousands of dollars, while the less fortunate and children gave their dimes and nickels. And the volunteers just kept coming; there was no further need to recruit them.

Ron Post and I had also become friends. I had even gotten used to his habit of saying, at the end of our occasional visits, "I love you, brother!" And while being hugged by a man much taller than myself always made me feel a bit silly, I found myself saying it back. I thought, if a Christian's first obligation is to model the love of Jesus Christ on Earth, as I had read, no one I knew did it better, in word and in action, than Ron Post. Even so, he took me by surprise one day when he called to say, "Brother, you really need to come with us on a mission. Will you go visit the poor people who live in garbage dumps in Mexico with us next month?"

We didn't go straight to Mexico City and its dumps. Ron had invited me and cameraman Tom Turner to follow the Northwest Medical Teams' five-hundredth mission—an incredible number when you consider how complex and difficult every trip actually is—to Oaxaca in southern Mexico, generally considered the country's poorest state.

We drove about an hour outside of the capital of Oaxaca City to a fully equipped medical clinic Post's volunteers had built in the rural countryside, several miles from the nearest town. It was staffed by medical and administrative personnel, all Mexicans and employed full-time by Northwest Medical Teams' in-country organization, Manos de Ayuda, which means "helping hands." In addition to the regular staff, teams of volunteers also regularly came here to provide much-needed medical care.

When the clinic was being built, critics told Post it was too far away from populated areas, and no one would come. They were wrong.

"Every morning, there'll be up to two hundred people who show up," Ron told me, "and they'll sit patiently all day long, waiting to see the doctor. Sometimes they will walk for a day or two out of the mountains, and then take a ten-hour bus ride to get here because someone said, 'Oh, if you go there, you can get help.'"

The team Ron had chosen for us to join—being the historic five-hundredth, and Ron having, perhaps left over from his rock-and-roll days, a flare for the dramatic—had come to help blind people see. When its volunteer doctors and nurses walked into the clinic on their first day, they received cheers and applause from the regular clinic staff members who had lined up to greet them. They would do nothing for the next week but cataract surgeries, but they would also change their patients' lives in extraordinary ways.

"These people have had no medical care, and they have gone to total blindness," explained Dr. Bob Laird, an ophthalmologist from Portland who, like all of the teams' volunteers, had flown to Mexico at his own expense and was using his own vacation time to do the work.

"The reason is obvious," said Dr. Laird. "When you see the people and realize they have so little and need so much. We know that if we were not here none of these people would see for the rest of their lives. We're in a position to be fortunate enough to give something back."

The patients had been brought to the clinic by relatives and loved ones, and as I talked to them through interpreters—sometimes two and three interpreters, since Oaxaca has so many indigenous languages—I learned that each and every one shared a common goal, not just to see again, but to become productive, to be able to go back to work.

Garcia Sanchez, an elderly but fit farmer, said he wanted to plant his beans and corn again; Vivian Martinez, eighty-five, wanted to cook, make tortillas; Fidel Perez, a deeply tanned and wrinkled eighty-two-year-old, wished to resume his basketmaking.

The surgical team worked on nine patients its first day, performing surgery that Dr. Laird explained would have been routine back home, but which was quite difficult here because the patients had been without medical care for years.

The following day, all nine were led back into the clinic by their relatives to have their bandages removed and to see if their surgeries were successful.

To commemorate the five-hundredth mission, the founder of the Northwest Medical Teams, his hands visibly shaking, was given the honor of removing the bandage of the first patient, Fidel Perez. Ron worked slowly and carefully, as the room fell silent. When the bandage came off, an attending nurse asked Fidel in his own language, "Can you see?" He didn't answer at first, perhaps startled by the brightness of the room. The question was repeated, "Can you see?" This time Fidel virtually shouted something in his native tongue which all present immediately understood: "Yes, I can see!" The room erupted into cheers, laughter, and ultimately tears, the other waiting patients and their relatives suddenly aware that perhaps a similar miracle could happen to them.

To my surprise, tears also ran down the cheeks of the medical people. I would have thought them used to such things, but what was taking place went well beyond normal surgical routine, and seeing the results of their own work in a way they had never seen before had a tremendous emotional impact.

I spoke to the youngest ophthalmologist on the team, Dr. Jennifer Lyons, who looked to me as if she might barely be out of college. She was crying softly.

"We all went into the medical profession to help people," she explained, "and I feel like I've failed in only doing this once so far. Everyone needs to do this a lot." It was Dr. Lyons's first mission with the teams, but I knew it wouldn't be her last.

Shirley Soderberg, a veteran operating room nurse at Willamette Falls Hospital in Oregon City, was on her fourteenth trip with the teams.

"Maybe we come here and at first feel, 'Oh, there's so many, how can we possibly help them all?'" she told our camera as the bandages continued to be removed from patients behind her. "But we can help them . . . one person at a time."

Ron Post, who had seen sight restored to Oaxaca patients many times before, admitted that he is moved to tears each and every time.

"There were nine people sitting there this morning who were blind yesterday," he said. "I guess if it were my own mother and father, I couldn't feel better."

The next day, photographer Tom Turner and I followed Fidel Perez, the basketmaker, as he returned to his own village. His countenance had changed completely and he walked with his head up, not downcast as we had seen him arrive at the clinic the day before. I wouldn't say that he ignored the villagers who greeted him with shouts and cheers, but he definitely moved with purpose through the village until he reached a pile of bamboo, pulling out a long shoot and cutting it with his sharp knife. Fidel sat down in the dust, a smile on his face. He was back at work, a basketmaker once again.

To make the best use of time and resources, each of the patients we saw at the Northwest Medical Teams clinic in Oaxaca had their sight restored in only one eye, not both, which was perfectly fine with them. It was as if they had been given their lives back. I would later learn that the actual, direct cost of one cataract surgery was only $137.

Before they left Oaxaca, the members of the ophthalmology team had restored sight to thirty-five patients. One of these, an ancient-looking woman whose skin had been deeply wrinkled by years of working in the hot sun, told the doctors as she left: "I have nothing to pay you, so God will pay you."

―――――――

I would have been happy to return home from Mexico at that point to produce our stories on the blind being given sight, but one of the reasons for our trip was to visit the dumps of Mexico City—the thought of which I'd been dreading for the last few days in Oaxaca. My news reporting had taken me to some pretty awful places in the world over the years, and I had conditioned myself to handle just about anything, but I couldn't imagine anything worse than visiting people who live in garbage, as Ron Post claimed many did.

At the time of our visit, Mexico City was already the world's largest city, with twenty-two million residents, a number that grew by three thousand or so each day. It was estimated that about six million of these were unemployed and had to find ways to somehow survive. Several hundred of them chose to do it by living in the Tultitlan landfill, about an hour out of the city, in shacks they had constructed from cardboard or discarded wood, whatever they could scavenge on the fringes of virtual mountains of reeking garbage.

"They came to Mexico City to work but found no jobs," Ron explained as we started to hike up one of the largest of the steaming mounds of trash and muck. "But there's no work and no welfare in Mexico, and they're hungry, so they come here to scavenge enough to eat."

Tom Turner and I both fought back revulsion as we continued on our way, Tom at one point taking video of hundreds of filthy tortillas that had been carefully placed on the ground next to a shack to dry in the sun. Emaciated dogs were picking through the tortillas, which were covered with flies. Everywhere we looked, the people who lived in the dump, called *pepenadores*, or "trash pickers," were digging through piles of refuse in their search for something to eat, as many children as there were adults.

"Won't the kids get sick from eating this stuff?" I asked Ron.

"They can," he said, "but even the air here is so bad the kids get sick from that. They ingest it into their stomachs and lungs."

Ron showed us a larger, more substantial shack, its plywood walls neatly whitewashed, a "clinic" that had been built in the dump by Northwest Medical Teams volunteers. The hope had been to build a more substantial clinic to treat the children of the dump, but this was all local officials would allow.

Inside, a Mexican doctor from Manos de Ayuda told us that she treated children primarily for stomach or respiratory illnesses caused by the pollutants that permeate the dump. "Yes," she said in answer to my question, "the children are sick mainly because of where they live." But she also said there was hope, that when she first came to work in the clinic every child she saw had worms, but with the medical care being provided in the shack, that problem was being turned around.

Ron Post looked at the faces of the children who were patiently waiting on benches to see the doctor and nurses.

"They're beautiful children—every one of them God's children," he said. He told us he'd been coming to the Mexico City dumps with his volunteers for ten years, and said each time he visits, he feels God's presence.

"Because God cares about these children," he explained. "He cares about their poverty. And all He does is ask us to give a helping hand to them."

After only a few hours—about all I could stand—we left the Tultitlan dump. I could not have been lower. Certainly no one could have a worse life than people who lived in and subsisted on garbage, and it was happening virtually next door to the wealthiest country in the world, my country. Ron consoled me and said I shouldn't feel bad, that the next day he would show us just what could be done for such people; how they could have their lives changed for the better, with just a little help.

The next morning found us about a half hour south of Mexico City, where the old Las Aguilas landfill had been closed and covered over for some years. It was mostly a large, open space now, but housing was being constructed on its fringes, and we met other volunteers who had traveled from churches in the United States to help build cinder-block houses.

We also met fifteen-year-old Marta Garcia, who was on her way to the sewing school that was started and run by Northwest Medical Teams. Ron told us that Marta used to live in the garbage, like the kids we saw at Tultitlan, but when she was five, NWMT volunteers took her to their daily breakfast program, where children were given regular, nutritious meals, the first they had ever known. Now Marta, in addition to her regular school studies, was learning to operate a sewing machine, and though she was very shy, she told us this would allow her to get a job one day, and would give her a chance in life. The same would be true for the other teenage girls we saw at the sewing school, and perhaps for many of the younger children we saw having breakfast being prepared and served by volunteers.

Next, we visited a sparkling new elementary school, the result of ten years of hard work by volunteers from the Northwest Medical Teams, Kiwanis Clubs, and other helping organizations from the United States. Tom photographed well-scrubbed, happy children, both in class and during recess, kids who also used to live in garbage.

Antonio Vazquez, in-country director of Manos de Ayuda, told us that many people believe the school is the finest in Mexico, a place that he said was built by love. "Many, many volunteers come to share their love with the children," Antonio said. "And this is the consequence, this school. It is love. It is love."

Ron Post looks at such developments in the neighborhood of the closed landfill—the new school, the breakfast program, the sewing classes—and wonders, if it can be done for the poorest of the poor in the garbage dumps of Mexico City, why can't the same be done for poor children all over the world?

"What an encouragement," he said while watching the children run and play at recess. "What an opportunity we have to change lives."

————

Since it began in 1979, Northwest Medical Teams has sent hundreds of teams and thousands of volunteers to scores of countries, to provide disaster relief, medical and dental care, supplies, food, and community development. In addition, each year the organization ships millions of dollars in medical and relief supplies to dozens more countries. In the Pacific Northwest, where the organization is based, NWMT mobile units take free medical and dental care directly to the homeless, to migrant workers, and to the poor of Oregon and Washington.

A few years ago, Ron Post retired from the teams, and he would be the last person to take credit for what the organization he founded has accomplished. Ron says it's the volunteers who deserve the credit, every one of whom, by the way, believes he or she benefited more from the work than those on the receiving end.

But the truth is, all of it began with just one man—a guy who was propelled from his easy chair by the evening news. That's why I think Ron Post is the single most important individual I've reported on in my career.

Because of him, none of us can look at any of the seemingly unsolvable problems in our world, from starvation to war, and say, "Hey, I'm just one person—there's nothing I can do."

Ron Post insists that anyone could do what he did and more, because as soon as he decided to step out of his own comfort zone, he found God there ready to help.

"His plan is for us to love one another as He loves us, and this means to care for one another," Ron has written. "He will give you everything you need to accomplish this, and the results for your life will be contentment and joy. Do we need anything else?"

CHAPTER SEVEN

What Is It and What Killed It?

A little inaccuracy sometimes
saves tons of explanation.
—*H. H. Munro ("Saki"),* **The Comments of Moung Ka,** *1924*

I HAD SEEN ALL I NEEDED to see of the decomposing whale and started to look for Doug, who was now back over by the sand dune getting cutaway shots of people sitting on a log.

Retrieving the tripod, I signaled for Doug to join me near where the official-looking guy in the silver hard hat was talking with some other ODOT workers. I needed a few minutes alone with him to see if he would talk to us on camera, which is never a sure thing. You would think that everyone would want to be on television, but I have learned that this is far from the case. Many times doing story work I have encountered people who, for whatever reason, have no interest in it at all. A guy responsible for dynamiting a whale might not want to talk about it on camera.

"Did you get shots of that bulldozer bringing in the dynamite?" I asked Doug, as he approached.

"Got it," he said.

"And those guys packing it under the whale?" I asked.

"More than we'd ever need," he said.

"Well, why don't we set up for an interview then," I advised. "I'm going to grab this guy in the hard hat as soon as he's free, he seems to be in charge. So be ready. Can you think of anything else we might need?"

"Not unless you want to talk to some of these other folks at some point," Doug answered. "I mean, there's a fair number of people who came out just to see what's going to happen."

I scanned the beach, from sand dune to ocean. Not counting the ODOT workers, I estimated there were now about fifty people hanging around, a few bold enough to walk out toward the whale for a closer look, but most hanging back on or near the dune, apparently just waiting for the blast. Occasional laughter and loud talking could be heard and there was definitely a sense of excitement in the air, the kind of anticipation felt by people awaiting darkness and a fireworks show on the Fourth of July.

If the ensuing years would bring criticism, even outrage, over the fact that a dead whale was blown up—and also shown on television in all of its strangeness—I wasn't aware of anyone that day questioning the wisdom of the plan. All present knew what was about to happen, and while I did overhear some conversations about whether it would work or not, most people seemed excited by the prospect of finding out. Doug's suggestion was a good one; maybe we would put the camera on a few of them later and ask for their comments.

"Hey, just one thing," Doug said as he started to move off to gather his gear.

"Has anyone said how this thing died?"

––––––––––

It's hard to remember all of the details, looking back at that day and those relatively few hours that we spent on the beach taking pictures and gathering information, more than three decades later. Some things I recall vividly—like the way the sky turned instantly red when tons of blubber were detonated and sent skyward—however, there are two essential facts that weren't given much attention when we went to Florence to cover the exploding whale. And frankly, I can't imagine why I didn't pin them down. I'm not embarrassed to say, all of these years later, that I should have done a better job as a reporter.

First, what kind of a whale was it? Someone on the beach, and I can't say with accuracy who, told me it was a Pacific gray whale, and that's how I reported it in my story.

That would certainly seem logical. As most Oregonians know, thousands of gray whales pass our coastline annually, migrating twelve thousand miles—from Alaska to the Baja Peninsula each Fall and back each Spring—the longest migration made by any marine mammal. Twice a year, thousands of curious people gather the full length of the Oregon coastline to see if they can get a glimpse of the largest mammals on earth as they swim by close enough to shore to be seen without binoculars. There are even volunteer guides posted to help visitors spot them.

Further, it is not uncommon for adult gray whales to be found washed up on Oregon and Washington beaches, as was the case twenty-five times in almost as many locations in the year 2000. Then again, other types of whales—beaked, pilot, or sperm, to name just a few of the seventy-six different varieties—also show up DOA on Oregon beaches from time to time.

If there was a marine biologist or whale expert to speak with on the beach in Florence that day in 1970, I didn't find one. It wasn't a problem for us, since our story was more about disposal and explosions than about whales or their habits, but my best recollection is that someone on scene, perhaps our ODOT official, informed me that the deceased was a gray whale. And so it didn't bother me to learn later that another news organization present that day, the *Siuslaw News* out of Florence, reported that it was a sperm whale. Oh well, I thought, some reporters can't even get the basic facts right.

As to Doug's question about what killed it, no one we talked to knew. I've learned since that the most common cause of whale deaths is, well, beaching—but while there are many theories on why whales beach themselves, no one knows for sure. They could be sick, or maybe their leader dies and they become lost, disoriented. But it was believed that this whale was dead when it washed up on shore.

Because they are mammals and breathe air, whales can drown, sometimes by becoming entangled in fishing nets. They can also be killed by hunters or poachers, die from pollution, or be impacted by a temporary lack of food supply. If an underfed whale begins the migration of thousands of miles (during which whales do not feed), he could end up with a fatally empty gas tank.

Our dead whale showed no wounds or signs of trauma. There had been no reports by fishermen of a whale being caught in their nets; there had been no word of hunters.

So what was it? Did this whale die of exhaustion, illness, starvation, or old age? Even though there wasn't an expert present to ask, I remain somewhat chagrined that my story, which would ultimately help spark worldwide interest in the episode for more than thirty years, didn't address what caused this whale to kick the old sand bucket. I just ignored this fact, which seems, in retrospect, a glaring omission.

———

I finally got a few minutes one-on-one with the man in the hard hat. His name was George Thornton, assistant district engineer for the Oregon Highway Division, and he did agree to an on-camera interview.

We interviewed differently back then. Today, because videotape cassettes are reusable and run thirty minutes or more, reporters can do most, if not all, of their questioning of subjects on camera. This also gives the interviewer a slight edge, because the subject is never quite sure when "the interview" has actually begun, or which answers will be used on the air.

In 1970, because we were shooting film and worked in constant fear of running out, reporters tended to ask all of their background questions off camera, and then direct the photographer to roll film for the actual interview, select portions of which would make the story and the newscast. This explains why we don't have an extensive interview with Mr. Thornton on file, which would tell us more about that day's events. I never saved story notes for long, so all that remains today that might constitute the "official" view are the comments by Mr. Thornton that were used in the story, and they are not extensive.

George Thornton was a slight, serious type—rather what you'd expect a highway engineer to be like. His bosses had apparently gone off on a long-planned deer-hunting trip, and he was left in charge of the whale disposal job. He answered my questions earnestly, pushing back his hard hat and looking down at the sand as he spoke, as if in serious concentration. There were no signs of nervousness I could discern, and he acted as if the interview was just a part of his job that day, though I wondered if he had ever been interviewed for TV before.

Why dynamite, I wanted to know. There wasn't an accepted, proven way of disposing of eight tons of whale, Mr. Thornton explained. Burying them didn't work—with the constant movement of the tides and seawater under the sand, they worked their way back to the surface. Towed to sea, it would likely wash back in. (I heard later that the whale had rotted so badly in three days it was doubtful it could have been "towed" at all, which is why dragging it up into the dunes for burial was considered, but not deemed a viable option.)

No less than the United States Navy had been consulted, Mr. Thornton said, and the only decision that could be made was to blow up the thing.

I told Doug we were ready for some on-camera questions, and he put us in place, photographing Mr. Thornton over my shoulder.

"Rolling," Doug said. I noticed that with this the highway engineer's demeanor changed not at all, there was still no nervousness, and he seemed still intent on answering my questions as best he could.

"Is this going to work?" I asked.

"Well, I'm confident that it will work," he said. "The only thing is we're not sure just exactly how much explosives it will take to disintegrate this thing so the scavengers, seagulls, and crabs and what not, can clean it up."

As the young producers on our staff today like to say, OH–MY–GOD! The engineer in charge of blowing up something that weighed eight tons wasn't sure how much explosive to use? That should have been my reaction, and my next question should have been, "then should we be doing this at all?" But I inexplicably let Mr. Thornton off the hook.

"Is there any chance it might be more than a one-day job?" I asked next. (Good grief, what was I thinking with that? Could I possibly have been pondering the chances of getting a night or two at the beach before returning to the everyday routine back in town?)

"Uh, if there's any large chunks left," said Thornton. "And, uh, we may have to do some other clean up. Possibly set another charge." The two "uhs" in only two sentences tell me that Mr. Thornton was caught by surprise by my moronic question as well.

And that was it. Those are the only words we would hear from an official—or from anyone else for that matter—in the original story on the exploding whale. Why all of the writers who have since viewed and commented on the story never questioned my failure to move the story in a more serious direction and challenge the state highway official, I've also never known.

Shortly after the interview, Doug and I were instructed to move a safe distance away from the blast site, and I decided there wasn't time to get comments on camera from any of the assembled bystanders. It was midafternoon, and we were on the edge of our deadline for getting this on the evening news. We were also getting real tired of smelling the whale, not at all anticipating how much worse it might get upon being blown open.

————

There were two daily newspapers in Oregon at the time, both Portland-based—the morning *Oregonian*, and the afternoon *Oregon Journal*. The November 13 edition of the *Oregonian* would describe the deceased as being a "forty-five-foot-long Pacific gray whale"; the *Oregon Journal* reported that it was a "California gray whale." Falling into my old habit of checking others to make sure my facts were correct, I figured the score was two to two: the two big guys, me and the

Oregonian, had it right, the two little guys, the *Oregon Journal* and the *Siuslaw News* (sperm whale), had it wrong.

At least that's what I thought until early in 2003. Doing some research on whales for this book, I e-mailed an expert I had met and interviewed many times on other subjects, a marine biologist named Bruce Mate. Based at the Hatfield Marine Science Center operated by Oregon State University in Newport, Dr. Mate may be the number one whale expert in the world. He might also be the best known, seen frequently in network and National Geographic documentaries.

To my great surprise, Dr. Mate wrote back that he had actually been there on the day they blew up the whale. He was a twenty-four-year-old graduate student and, at the time, most likely the only person in Oregon studying marine mammals. He was working on his Ph.D. project, which concerned the migration habits of sea lions, but had heard about the whale in Florence and had driven up from Coos Bay to see it, arriving about thirty minutes before detonation.

"I asked if they would give me time to get into the animal, retrieve its stomach contents, gonads, and such," Bruce related. "If you have these things you can tell if it died from trauma, its breeding habits, and much more." But the highway division workers would have little to do with him.

"Their response was, 'take a few measurements and then move back, sonny, because we're about to blow this mess up,'" he explained. "I also had some experience with explosives before then and could pretty much predict the outcome, but it was obvious to me that the input of a twenty-four-year-old 'kid' was not going to carry much weight."

When authorities moved those assembled a quarter mile back from the blast site, Mate moved back a half mile to see what would happen next.

"I watched the entire process," he recalled, "including the rain of rancid whale oil over the crowd. What a scene!"

And so, finally, more than three decades later, I had found my expert. After studying his e-mail, I called Bruce Mate at his home to see if I could get my other questions pinned down—the type of whale and how it died.

"We do not know the cause of death and never will," he said. It might have been different had Mate been allowed to do his collecting that day.

What kind of whale was it?

"It was a very large, male sperm whale," Dr. Mate stated, "which most often roam as solitary individuals. Such individual strandings of large, male sperm whales are not at all common, especially off Oregon. There's been only one other in the thirty-four years I have been keeping tabs on these matters."

I thanked Dr. Mate for the information and hung up the phone, sitting quietly for several minutes to contemplate how badly I and everyone else missed the importance of the entire episode. Today, the rare beaching of a sperm whale would likely attract the attention of environmentalists and reporters from far and wide, with experts like Bruce Mate being allowed to gather whatever information they thought necessary to help us learn more about how and why it had happened. The whale's disposal, the only story we covered, would likely be a small addendum

I also thought of the unknown reporter from the *Siuslaw News* who had correctly identified the species of whale. Certainly I should have known that a journalist working on the Oregon Coast would have more knowledge about such things than I would, but I wonder if he or she ever saw our television story and thought, "Those television guys can't even get the basic facts right."

CHAPTER EIGHT

What Happens When You Don't Quit

I think what I represent is achieving what you want in life.
It's a matter of attitude. Some people have a negative
attitude, and that's their disability.
—*Marla Runyan in* Runners World
(legally blind runner and Olympian), 2003

LOCAL TV TYPES are frequently asked to give talks to various groups and organizations that are always in need of speakers. Because I've spent nearly my entire career anchoring the news and hosting talk shows in Portland, I've gotten my fair share of invitations. However, I try to keep a good perspective about being so honored—if I drove the parcel post truck or painted houses for a living I'd never be asked.

It's fun to talk for twenty minutes or so about what is or isn't happening in television news and to share a blooper story or two, but for me the most entertaining part of these forays into the community is the requisite question-and-answer period. I always seem to be amused by what comes up, what subjects viewers are interested in learning more about.

Invariably, it's the whale, a subject I normally don't address during my prepared remarks because audiences seem to enjoy it more when one of their own brings it up.

"Hey Paul, aren't you the guy who blew up that whale?" is the way it's most frequently addressed.

I always find it a curious way to put the question because, of course, they certainly know I wasn't, that I just happened to be there at the time. (It's not just luncheon or banquet attendees either: I got a call from the governor's office last fall, his chief of staff teasing me that another whale had washed ashore, and they needed me on the coast right away to blow it up.)

There are always a few in the audience, and I routinely check to see, who haven't heard the story, and I'm then compelled (by those who have) to share it, if only in brief, yet again. This gives those in the know a chance to enjoy the reaction of those hearing it for the first time, and their enthusiasm tends to charge audience response to a very old story.

After all of these years, I can't begin to imagine why the whale remains so interesting to so many people, but I can tell you it does. And to this day, after speaking in detail about the incident, I will be approached by a handful of people from each audience who have more questions and who want to know how they can get copies of the video.

———

Of all the groups that I speak to, my favorites are those made up of young people—students, athletic teams, and also kids with a serious interest in journalism. This is due only in part to the fact that they are too young to have heard about the whale and are not apt to ask about it. More importantly, I relish sharing with them an invaluable message learned from the hundreds of inspiring people I've reported on: if you want to succeed in life, just don't quit. It's all you need to know.

To prove it, I often begin by relating a personal experience. One day near the outset of a personal fitness campaign—I badly needed to lose about thirty pounds—I was swimming laps in the local Y pool. I could only go about two lengths without gassing out, having to cling to the side while the real lap swimmers went back and forth, effortlessly.

But on this day, my mind was deep in thought on something other than swimming and I forgot to stop; I just kept going until I had completed a quarter mile, eighteen lengths. Soon after that, each time I returned to the pool I swam a full mile, and ultimately, my weight loss campaign was successful. Success came only because I didn't stop.

I took the same attitude into marathon running next, then to triathlons, and as a result, can honestly tell young people that they don't have to be the strongest, the fastest, the smartest, or the best looking to succeed in life. All it takes is not quitting. (It's a fact in marathon running that a person who runs at an 8.5-minute-per-mile pace, about twice as slow as the fastest runners, will pass half the field before completing the 26.2 mile distance.)

Personal experiences aside, I like to tell kids about my favorite nonquitters, the many inspirational people I've written about for our newscasts.

Some are surprised to learn that John Callahan, the nationally syndicated cartoonist, has found great success despite being paralyzed in a car accident.

Most have never heard of Mildred Davy, still a very popular radio talk show host at the age of ninety.

I tell them about Bruce Munson or Mark Francis, men who craft beautiful cabinets despite being blind; or Robert Clark, an insurance man who became Oregon's first African-American PGA golf professional despite some pretty big odds against him.

The kids love hearing about the Washington State School for the Deaf football team, whose members can't hear their quarterback call signals, but they're as quick off the ball as any high school football team; about Dale Etna Powers, who was well into her eighties before realizing her dream of riding horseback in parades like a rodeo queen; or Bob Anderson, who went from being a Portland school's most popular janitor to one of its best-liked teachers.

I tell them about the Phame Academy and its developmentally delayed actors and actresses who do full musical productions; Bruce

Brennan, a deaf pilot who was once told he would never be able to fly his own plane, but does; and Desi Stone, a stay-at-home mom/filmmaker.

In every case, and I can cite hundreds more, these people achieved their goals and met with unbelievable success for one reason: they didn't quit.

And if my student groups still don't buy it, I tell them about Art Pease.

———

I first read about Art in an out-of-town newspaper. The short item reported that he was a twenty-three-year-old developmentally delayed runner who, due to some prerace confusion, actually ran a full marathon by mistake. I didn't believe it possible, so I placed a call to his family in the town of Milton-Freewater, a small farming community in Eastern Oregon.

"It's true," Art's father, Charlie, chuckled over the phone, "he ran the whole thing—all twenty-six-point-two miles of it." After some conversation and considerable urging on my part, Charlie agreed to bring Art to Portland so that we could tell his story on the news.

Art was part of a Special Olympics group that had trained to enter the five-mile run of the Portland Marathon, considered among the best-organized multirace events in the United States. But there was a mix-up on race morning when one of the athletes became lost just before the start of the five-miler. Charlie Pease, a middle school athletic director and Special Olympics volunteer coach, told his son Art to stay put in the race's busy staging area while he rushed off to find the missing runner.

But minutes later, a cannon boomed to signal the start of the full, 26.2-mile marathon. Art, thinking it was the start of his five-mile race, jumped from the curb into the crowd of runners and took off. He had come to Portland, after all, to run.

When we got together weeks after the race, it wasn't difficult to re-create the story on video. We recorded several scenes of Art running alone over the marathon course, and of Charlie and his wife, Virginia, driving their car through the city as if searching for their son, as they had done on marathon day. Our weekend news had covered the marathon, so it was a simple matter of editing the actual marathon scenes with our new video of the Peases, a pretty simple re-creation. We weren't trying to fool viewers into thinking they were watching race-day video. We just wanted give them the idea of what it must have looked like.

When we sat down in a park on the marathon course to do the interview work, I took an immediate liking to Art. He was a wiry young guy with short hair, a constant tight-lipped expression on his face, and a straight-ahead, no-nonsense way of talking. He seemed to smile slightly at some of my questions and look off for answers to others, but he concentrated mightily on his answers, delivering them with few words and intense directness.

I asked him what he was thinking when his anticipated five-mile run just kept going on and on. "Getting kind of tired," Art deadpanned. Off camera, Charlie and Virginia looked at each other and laughed, kindly and openly.

They had told me earlier how Art had come to their family. With five children of their own, they'd adopted Art when he was seven years old. He was an abused child who authorities believed had spent the first several months, if not years, of his life actually tied to his crib by his ankle. Charlie thought it might be why Art's left foot turned out noticeably when he ran, something I noticed when we took the video of his running.

Art joined the Pease family at Thanksgiving time, and on one of their first outings together they visited friends for dinner. Art seemed cheerful but upon arriving at the other family's house, lingered behind, obviously not wanting to go inside.

"It was raining," Charlie said, "and Art just stood out in the yard looking up, letting the raindrops hit his face and smiling. Virginia and I kind of figured right then, this kid had never been outside before." It was later learned that if he was taken anyplace as a small child, for reasons unknown, he was kept covered up on the floor of the backseat of a car.

As our interviewing continued, it was easy to see how much these three loved and cared for one another: Art, athletic and thin, good-natured but quiet; his parents, outgoing, outsized people—quick to smile and laugh, proud of their son and of his achievements. They sat nearby, beaming, as I asked Art questions on camera, openly chuckling when his answers were unusual or unexpected. If I'd been uneasy or uncomfortable doing stories with developmentally delayed people in the past, the Peases taught me by their actions that I needn't be again. They were perhaps the most accepting people I had ever met.

"When did you realize you were in the big race, not the five-miler?" I asked Art.

"Out on the bluff by U of P, where the run turns around, I saw everyone had different-colored numbers than mine," he said. The marathon was run on an out-and-back course, which turned around at the halfway point near the University of Portland in the north part of town. When Art started running back toward the start and passed slower runners still going out, he noticed their marathon numbers were a different color than his. If he had wondered what was going on before, now he had to know he was in the big run.

Art was about fifteen miles into the marathon when race officials finally spotted the accidental marathoner. They had spent hours trying to find Art in a field of four thousand runners, with a crowd of seventy thousand or so on hand to watch.

"We caught up with him and asked what he wanted to do," recounted Les Smith, Portland attorney and longtime volunteer race director. "He said, 'I want to keep going,' and away he went." Art appeared to be doing well, and wasn't in any distress, so race officials let him run on. They closely monitored him for the remainder of the race, and reported back periodically to Charlie and Virginia that their son was still running and doing fine.

Before my photographer and I finished our work with the Pease family, Charlie casually mentioned something that blew us away and would absolutely make our story—he had actual video of Art running in the marathon. It turned out that a woman from Washington state who read the same article I had realized she had run most of the race near Art. Her husband had videotaped her at several locations, and Art was in the background in many scenes.

Art could be seen running in many of the shots, plodding along mile after mile, head down, gutting it out. But even better, the video showed him actually completing the marathon, crossing the finish line with a look of iron determination on his face, four hours and eighteen minutes after he'd begun, a very respectable time. We intercut these scenes with our own, and our story was complete.

Les Smith, the marathon director, also appeared in the story, confirming that Art's achievement was unquestionably a first—no one had ever run 26.2 miles by accident before. "It's phenomenal," Les exclaimed. "The question is, how did he do it?"

"Just kept running," was Art's short, honest answer in the story. And that's certainly what all marathoners do to complete one of the most grueling tests in sports—it's just that every one else plans and trains for months to do it. Art, who in addition to his regular running also lifted weights and rode his bike to and from his job at a Milton-Freewater fruit-packing plant, had apparently trained enough—also an accidental cross-trainer.

To end our story, I asked Art if he could explain how it felt when he finished, achieving what most would consider a lifetime goal. What was he thinking at that wonderful, crowning moment?

"Finally finished the race," he said in a monotone. There was more laughter off camera from his mom and dad. Did he plan on running another marathon in the future? I wanted to know.

"Yep. Going to train for it next time, though," he said. That sent Charlie and Virginia over the edge in laughter. Soon all of us, Art, me, and my photographer included, were laughing uncontrollably. Our interview was over, and we were all happy.

In retrospect, I think the real story may not have had so much to do with Art finishing the marathon by mistake as it was about his special, loving family. They supported and accepted one another in ways only people with special-needs children can understand, and

I hoped that message would come across in our story about the Peases.

In the years since, we've updated Art's story many times. We've taken video of his training runs in the desolation of Eastern Oregon: Art running long stretches of lonely, straight roads, Charlie and Virginia following slowly behind in the family station wagon, supplying water and moral support when needed. At last count, Art had finished twenty-seven marathons, including Boston—twenty-six of them on purpose. In 1995, he was named International Special Olympics Athlete of the Year, and he's married now, to Jennifer Lynn, also a Special Olympian.

We've become friends over the years. He's traveled to Portland so we could run together in the New Year's Eve race my television station sponsored, and we see each other annually at the Portland Marathon awards ceremony. I'm often the announcer at this event, having the privilege of presenting Art and his Special Olympics teammates with their medals. Art and I always hug and share tears of joy at such times, Charlie and Virginia invariably nearby, beaming proudly.

The youth groups I talk to always seem to love the story, and of the thousands of feature subjects I've covered in my career, Art Pease is my number one, all-time favorite. Maybe someday at one of my luncheon speeches the first question from the audience will be about the accidental marathoner instead of the exploding whale. I'm still waiting for that to happen, and I won't quit.

CHAPTER NINE

Having a Blast at the Beach

The goal of all inanimate objects is to resist man and
ultimately defeat him.
    —*Russell Baker, "The Plot Against People," 1978*

THERE WAS LITTLE LEFT for us to do but wait for the explosion. We
did need to shoot a brief opening stand-up—that's when the reporter
looks into the camera and sets the scene—but since I hadn't yet figured
out what I wanted to say, the stand-up would have to wait. It wouldn't
take long once I had my thoughts in order.

The highway division workers had finished packing the dynamite
around the whale, most of it on the side facing shore so it would be
blown toward the ocean. They had also strung wire from the whale
several hundred yards up into the dunes where, I guessed, the
detonator was located.

George Thornton had informed everyone still on the beach—many
of the bystanders had moved away and taken up positions to watch
what would happen next—that they needed to move a quarter of a
mile away to the south.

I was disappointed with this information, not really knowing what
we, or our cameras, would be able to see from such a distance. I tried
to determine how far a quarter mile was. I thought about when I
covered drag racing stories; how well could I see a car after it had
traveled a quarter mile away?

"We should be okay from there," Doug advised when I raised the question with him. "Of course we can use the zoom lens on the sound camera, but I don't know how much you'll be able to see with the silent camera."

I decided against pressing our case for being closer, but I did ask Mr. Thornton how we would know when to start our cameras from such a distance. He said another worker would signal us by dropping a red flag. Doug shrugged his shoulders and nodded at this, indicating once again that this should be okay for our purposes. I trusted his judgment in all cases when it came to getting pictures.

We gathered up our gear and started to move away from the whale, stopping only briefly so Doug take a few shots of a sheriff's deputy telling an older couple they'd have to move farther back. They were sitting on a log on the beach and didn't appear happy about giving up their viewing position, only a football field or so away from where the whale rested. Later, they'd be thankful.

We shot our stand-up. Television reporters today frequently introduce their prepackaged stories live and on location, but in 1968 the only opportunity a reporter had to appear on camera in the field was through the filmed stand-up. They were tricky to do, because they were shot out of context, with the actual story being written and narrated later. Whatever information was presented on camera had to match the story's eventual attitude; in short, the stand-up had to stand up later.

Doug placed me before the camera, positioning the real star of our story over my right shoulder so that I could indicate the dead whale's presence with a slightly affected nod of my head. I didn't actually write my stand-up but had a couple of thoughts in mind, which I simply "talked" to the camera, as if it were a single viewer. It wasn't detailed information, just that the highway division had a problem on its hands in trying to dispose of an eight-ton whale. It served only to set up our story and, of course, place me at the scene.

Doug confirmed that my brief words were generic enough to work later, and we moved on.

After hiking up the dune to our designated spot, we set our gear down and got ready to shoot the explosion. Doug placed the big Auricon sound camera on its tripod and told me there was still plenty of film left in its 400-ft magazine, but that we needed to put a new 100-ft roll of film in the silent camera I'd be using.

Our plan was that I'd shoot the blast in slow motion, which required the film to move through the camera approximately twice as fast as normal, so we'd better have a full roll of film to work with. (Looking back, I find it curious that we'd decided to double-shoot the explosion and to use slow-motion photography, I guess for use like a replay in a football game. Did we actually think that the innards of a whale blowing up would be something viewers would want to see in slow motion?)

I looked around at our viewing spot, which I decided might be fine after all. We were set up only a hundred yards or so north of where we'd left the borrowed car, so it would be easy to shoot the final element of our story and make a dash for the airport.

Since it was going on four o'clock, we no longer felt pressed to get our story back for the early evening newscast, but it would be good to get out of there and on our way home immediately after this was over. We would probably have to work late to produce the story for our eleven o'clock news, and it was beginning to look like a long day.

The beach had grown quiet, conversation had died down, and the only sound was that of the breakers, perpetually rolling up the sand. I looked toward the whale and could see no activity, the small bulldozer having been removed from the site, it's work done (at least for now).

My thoughts went to my bosses back in the Channel 2 newsroom, who must be wondering by now what had happened to us, and our story. We had left first thing in the morning with the understanding that there would be plenty of time to get our piece back for the early news. There wasn't any way for us to check in from the beach to update our situation. (It's curious how times change. Back then, we considered it a problem not being able to communicate with the newsroom from the field. Reporters today, who are in constant touch with their managers by cell phone, would likely be thrilled not to have to deal with the incessant changes of plans by producers and assignment editors. Improved communication has not necessarily made reporting easier.)

Our bosses probably thought Doug and I were out having fun again, maybe sitting around after the explosion, having a few beers with the highway division guys. I wished we were. And frankly, as we neared the countdown to the whale's detonation, I was growing increasingly nervous—not about the explosion itself, but my own ability to capture it on film with Doug's camera.

———

For a brief period in 1969, I did realize my dream of working in sports journalism. The station's sports director had moved on to another job in broadcasting, and I was assigned to take over his duties doing nightly sportscasts on our early and late news programs.

To my disappointment, I found that I didn't like working in sports at all. It was too much dessert, and it made work out of sports. I soon stopped reading the sports section every morning—a lifelong routine—because it seemed like going to work early.

And while on the job, I could never see an entire game—maybe a quarter of basketball, a few innings of baseball—before having to return to the station to prepare my segment for the next newscast.

It was clearly a case of be careful of what you want most in life because you just might get it. And the worst part of it was that I had to film most of the sports events myself—there being too few photographers to go around—and I was terrible at it.

The photographers were kind enough to give me ongoing instruction in how to operate the two silent film cameras commonly used at the time, the Bolex and the Bell and Howell, but I just never got it. The Bell and Howell was difficult to use because you could not focus it by looking through the viewfinder; the shooter had to estimate the distance to the subject, and then turn the camera's turret to line up the correct lens, or in the alternative, focus it through a tiny peephole on the side of the camera. I couldn't see through the peephole, and I was inept at judging distances, so what I shot with this camera was frequently out of focus and unusable.

My worst experience on this count came one night when I had to shoot the Portland Buckaroos playing a Western Hockey League game at the Memorial Coliseum.

I had wasted nearly all of the first roll of film trying to get a goal. That's all I needed for my story; if I had just one goal on film, I could write my script around it and tell the rest of the game's story over generic footage. But having already shot one hundred feet of film, I wasn't positive I'd captured either of the two goals the Bucks had scored in their first period of play. I'd have to reload the camera and stay for the second period.

If I had trouble focusing the Bell and Howell, I was even worse at loading it. Rather than attempt it in the pressroom where professional photographers from the other stations might observe my ineptitude, I went high into the arena's end zone seats where I could sweat through changing film in isolation. But in attempting to place the new roll of film in the camera, I accidentally dropped it, the small black reel falling between the seats and onto the floor beneath the bleachers far below.

I had no other choice but to go under the grandstand to try to recover the film. It was dark under there, and as I searched through the discarded soda cups, popcorn boxes, and other assorted litter, my hope was I could find the film before someone saw me, a major market sportscaster, sorting through the trash at a pro hockey game.

"Hey, what are you doing under here?" a voice from behind a flashlight beam called out. A Coliseum security guard had found me and was coming my way. "You can't be under here—I'm going to have to ask you to go back to your seat."

I didn't even try to explain. I drove back to the station and made do with the film I had—there was one slightly out of focus scoring play I was able to edit into the story. I decided that night, for the second time in my brief career, that sports journalism was not for me.

———

It was growing chilly on the sand dune. I checked with Doug to make sure my camera was wound and ready to go. Doug explained that because the Bolex I was using was set for slow motion, and would be exposing film at about sixty frames per second versus the standard twenty-four, I should wait until the last possible moment before I began filming. The camera was hand wound and would only operate for five seconds before it would need to be wound again.

"Don't worry too much because I'll have us covered with the sound camera," Doug instructed. "But try not to start early with that thing."

We both looked to the north where we saw a highway division worker standing alone two or three dunes away. He raised a small, red flag, and held it above his head.

I could hear that Doug had started his camera rolling—it was set on the whale—but I hadn't started mine yet. I held the Bolex at about shoulder level, also pointed in the direction of the whale. Doug wasn't looking through his viewfinder, we were both intently watching the man with the flag a quarter-mile away.

It was very quiet. There were other onlookers not far from us, but there was no talking. There had been hundreds of gulls on the beach all day, squawking in apparent anticipation of a major meal, but now they were silent as well. All I could hear were the distant breakers and Doug's camera, the sixteen-millimeter film steadily working its way through the big Auricon. I wondered if Doug should turn his camera off; we didn't want to use up what film was left before the explosion took place, and there was no telling how long the worker would hold the flag in the air.

Then he dropped it.

———

At first, there was nothing particularly surprising or significant about the blast; it looked like any explosion commonly seen in action adventure films, V-shaped and forceful, with great amounts of matter shooting rapidly upward. But as the material filled the sky and seemed to momentarily hang in the air, there were a few things that gave this explosion an odd look and feel.

The first was its color, the airspace directly above where the whale had been turned a deep crimson. Explosions in the movies usually look like a blast of fire and smoke, this one more resembled a mighty burst of tomato juice.

The sound was also odd, though not at first. A tremendous boom caught up with us a second or two after detonation, but after several more seconds, we began hearing what sounded like something hitting the ground around us. One or two at first, then several at once, a series of hollow "thunk" noises, like the spatter of heavy rain falling on pavement, only somehow more serious and with greater volume. At first, I wasn't sure what to make of it.

But as I looked in the distance to see stuff from the explosion fall back to the ground near the blast site, I could definitely make out large, formless chunks of something coming down, pieces of—oh my God, don't tell me—blubber. That had to be what was falling near us as well, the thunk, thunk, thunk all around us now. It had been blown all the way to us. We were in a massive blubber shower.

I heard a male voice nearby. It was sing-songy, and went, "Ooooooooh Nooooo," but with laughter on the end. I recognized the voice—it was Doug, who had backed slightly away from his camera's viewfinder to take in the entire picture for himself. He sounded at once amused, in awe, and surprised.

The next voice I heard was a woman's, obviously a stern mother chiding her child.

"All right, Fred, you can take your hands out of your ears now," she ordered. And then, from the same voice, in a more concerned yet contemplative tone: "Here come pieces of . . ." her voice suddenly trailed off and I couldn't quite make out her last word, but it sounded like a simple curse, "Hell!"

The next thing I knew, Doug and I were running. I don't recall any communication between us, I don't remember Doug removing the camera from its tripod or our picking up any gear, I only remember this tremendous urge to get away. The thunking noise, whale meat hitting the ground all around us, had not decreased in intensity. We were at full sprint, charging through the sand down the backside of the sand dune.

I've always considered myself fortunate and blessed not to have gone to war in my life. Nearly all of the young men I received artillery training with at Fort Sill, Oklahoma, were sent to Vietnam, many making the ultimate sacrifice for their country. As a member of the National Guard and not the regular Army, I was fortunate to be able to return home after being trained.

But if anything ever gave me the sense of what it might be like to be in combat and under fire, it was the day Doug Brazil and I ran in terror to escape the blubber shrapnel. We could hear it pounding into the earth on all sides, both of us fully realizing that should either of us be struck by a sizeable piece, it could be all over. What an ignominious way to go, taken out by a flying piece of dead whale meat.

We had almost made it to the parking area when, to our amazement, there was another, smaller explosion. We both skidded to a stop in the sand because this blast hadn't come from behind us, in the direction of the whale; it seemed to be ahead of us, only several yards away. Doug and I looked at each other in confusion, trying to understand what was happening. Fortunately, the sound of blubber hitting the ground had now all but ceased.

I was next aware of the people around us, who I realized must have also been running away. Now, most everyone was walking, and in the same direction, to see what had caused the second explosion in the parking lot.

It was a nearly new Oldsmobile Regal. A piece of blubber maybe six inches thick, about the size of an end table, had landed on the left rear corner of the Oldsmobile's roof. It completely flattened the roof, blowing out its windows and showering the area with broken glass. It didn't appear anyone had been in the vehicle when it was struck, and no one we could see in the immediate area had been injured. The Oldsmobile, however, looked to be a goner.

Two things stick in my mind about that very peculiar day and the incredible experience of watching a sperm whale being blown up. The first is the smell. Doug and I have talked about this repeatedly over the years, deciding that there simply are no words to describe it. It was overpowering and stayed in our nostrils for several days after the incident. I can still recall it instantly, as if it still lives somewhere within, ready to return with all of its rottenness.

I used to play golf at a course located not far from a rendering plant, and the strange meat smells from that operation that often blew in our direction always put me in mind of the exploding whale, but even that smell had nowhere near the intensity. There's just nothing that comes close to the aroma of decomposing whale guts and blood and blubber, blown open with the force of dynamite and sprayed all over you.

The other thing I often think about is the film I shot that day with the silent camera. Doug and I have never seen it and no matter how hard we try, we can't recall what we did with it or figure out where it might have ended up.

One of Doug's theories is that the camera ran out of "wind" before the actual explosion, and he, being the professional and all, is probably right. I've chosen just to accept the fact that I'll never know what happened to that footage, filing it away in my mind somewhere near the roll of film the big sportscaster lost at the hockey game. I'm not sure I'd want to see that mess in slow motion, anyway.

CHAPTER TEN

Mind over Matter

We don't stop playing because we get old.
We get old because we stop playing.
—*Leroy Satchel Paige,* Satchell Sez, 2001

ONE OF THE SPECIAL THINGS about feature reporting is that it can allow you to live your dreams, like the time I got to try out for the Pittsburgh Pirates.

It happened at their spring training camp, dubbed "Pirate City," located on the Gulf Coast near Bradenton, Florida. I was there to do stories on players who might be assigned to Pittsburgh's Triple-A affiliate at the time, the Pacific Coast League's Portland Beavers. I also wanted to produce a piece on some kid from Oregon who might be trying out for the National League team.

The Pirates were the last team in major league baseball willing to give anyone who showed up at training camp a shot at making the bigs. If you could get to Florida, they'd actually let you try out to become a professional baseball player. Each spring, young ballplayers would come from all over the country for the opportunity, many hitchhiking great distances and sleeping on the beach to do it. What a great setup for a story, and my hope was to profile some big league wannabe from Oregon.

But because there were no walk-ons from the Northwest that spring, someone in the organization suggested that I take a run at it. I thought, why not? I was in my thirties but had played high school ball, and actually believed back then that I could play pro ball. (I also thought I could be an astronaut if that didn't work out.) Such youthful thinking aside, if George Plimpton could make a career out of partici- patory journalism—trying sports he couldn't do and then writing about it—I could do one story on myself trying to make the majors.

Just putting on the uniform was a thrill. This was around the time that the Pirates had launched the idea of having several different sets of shirts and pants that they could mix and match in various uniforms, all combinations of white, yellow, and black, some solid, some pinstripes. The uniform I was given was the traditional pinstripe version, top and bottom, and I must have spent a half-hour alone in the locker room looking at myself in the mirror. Maybe I didn't have the physique of Pirates stars Willie Stargell or Dave Parker, but I think I could have passed for a player. Okay, maybe a player-coach.

My tryout was conducted by a couple of pretty good names in baseball, Branch Rickey III, the scion of one of the game's pioneers, and Murray Cook, future general manager of the New York Yankees. I was tested in two different drills, the first of which was a timed run from the batter's box to first base. To my amazement, Rickey informed me that my time was only 1.5 seconds slower than the National League average.

"How about that?" I exclaimed to no one in particular.

"That's light-years too slow," Rickey advised, my lack of speed all but eliminating the need to do the other drill. But Branch said that I shouldn't feel bad, that his taking a look at the young ballplayers who showed up uninvited, in most cases, was merely a courtesy.

"Our organization evaluates so many thousands of players," Rickey explained, "we can usually tell if a young pitcher's got it just by how he walks to the mound. But we let them throw anyway."

Rickey and Cook put me through the other test—throwing from position—then gave me the so-long speech: "You just don't have what the Pittsburgh Pirates are looking for in a player right now. But we'd like nothing more than for you to prove us wrong, catch on with another team and come back and beat us. So good luck and thanks for your interest in our ball club."

I'd heard them say the same words to several kids that week in Florida, and now they were saying them to me, as my photographer recorded it all, a story I would keep for life on my personal reel.

———————

The story was actually better because I had failed so badly at trying to make the Pittsburgh Pirates; it had pathos, some humor, and a message, that the aging fan who finds himself thinking he could take the field and play with the professional athlete, in any sport, is just dreaming.

Even so, I once did a story on an elderly car salesman who swore he could step into the batter's box and hit major league pitching today. This guy had some experience to back up that claim, and I came to believe he could do it, too. As a matter of fact, of all the athletes I've reported on in my career, Arthur Lee Wilson would have to be my favorite.

———————

I first saw Artie when he was playing in an old-timers game in a dust-blown Single-A park in Bend, Oregon. He was much older than the other former players, but there was no mistaking his grace and elegance on the ball field, the way he ran with ease, threw on target, and swung his bat as if it were second nature. He was thin and fit as a fungo even though he was going on eighty years of age. As I watched him turn double plays and effortlessly stroke base hits, I noticed the other players seemed to defer to him, an acknowledgment of his incredible career in baseball.

Artie may have been the best infielder never to make the major leagues. Well, actually he did get to the big show for a cup of coffee—nineteen games with the New York Giants—but baseball's color barrier had held him back, and he didn't arrive at the Polo Grounds until 1951, a thirty-year-old rookie.

Born in Springfield, Alabama, in 1920, Artie was at one time the player-manager of the Negro American League's much-heralded Birmingham Black Barons. He was a shortstop and an excellent lead-off hitter, winning the league's batting crown in 1947 and 1948 with averages of .377 and .402.

Moving to the Pacific Coast League in 1949, he was the league leader in stolen bases (47), and won another batting title (.348), becoming the first player in PCL history to do so without hitting a single home run.

A left-handed slap-hitter, Wilson sent everything to the opposite field, causing one opposing manager to shift all of his players to the left side of the diamond when Artie came to bat, even the first baseman.

"It didn't matter," Artie recalled. "I still hit it to left field, and the ball landed between 'em."

It's impossible to know what kind of career Artie could have had in the major leagues had he made it as a young man. His quick hands and feet made him a master of the double play; he was generally considered the best shortstop in the black leagues in his time, helping the Black Barons win three pennants.

Lefty O'Doul, who hit .350 lifetime in the big leagues, got a good idea of what kind of player Artie was one day after watching him turn four double plays in a double-header against his San Francisco team in the PCL.

"You don't see shortstop played better by anybody than you saw today," the Seals' manager told reporters. "I spent a few years in the majors, but I never saw anything like the exhibition Wilson staged."

Upon meeting Artie, a soft-spoken, distinguished-looking gentleman with a perfect, white goatee, I learned of his love for another game, golf. We agreed to play at Artie's home course, a nifty little par-3 affair in Portland called "The Children's Course." It had been developed by local benefactors to give inner-city kids a place to learn life's lessons through golf, and Artie spent a lot of time there. When he wasn't at his full-time job selling new cars at a nearby Lincoln-Mercury dealership, he was at the Children's Course mentoring and helping youngsters who had discovered golf.

"Have you ever played with Artie?" asked one of the regulars as I warmed up, waiting for him to arrive. "If you haven't, watch out—when he's chipping, it's like he's putting, he thinks he can make everything, and usually does."

So warned, we agreed to play nine holes for a dollar, which became our standard bet in many future rounds. Artie missed the first two greens with his approach shots, but hit the pin both times with his chips. On the third hole, he chipped into the cup from off the green as if it were routine, confirming what the local told me and one of my long-held beliefs: a good athlete is a good athlete, whatever the sport. But what seemed to take Artie Wilson to a higher plane in competition was his incredibly positive attitude.

I came to love playing with him. He did think he was capable of making every shot, and he had a wonderful approach to golf, just seeming to let what happened happen and enjoying the results. When he hit a bad shot, and especially if I'd needle him about it a little, he always had the same curious response.

"That's all right," he'd say in a sing-song way, with his voice going way up on "all," as if reminding himself that he could overcome whatever brief setback had presented itself. I began to wonder if such a response—and maybe it was a philosophy, an accepting, "that's all right" attitude—had gotten Artie through some daunting situations in life.

And as we played, I loved hearing the stories about his days with the Black Barons, or playing in the Pacific Coast League, the teams I grew up watching in Portland. Each round of golf with Artie was like a living history lesson, and I couldn't get enough.

"Best pitcher you ever faced?" I'd ask. "Satchel Paige, by far," Artie said without hesitation, "and the best hitter was Josh Gibson. No one could hit like he could, ever." Then, he would take a stance, and show me Gibson's incredibly powerful swing, it's distinctive arc burned into his memory, Artie recognizing greatness when he saw it all of those years ago.

With little prompting, he'd relate stories about barnstorming with black all-stars in the South, his teams made up of fabled players with colorful names like "Cool Papa" Bell and "Double Duty" Radcliffe, the latter given his nickname by the great writer Damon Runyon because of his ability to pitch the first game of a doubleheader and catch the second.

Artie told me about playing ballgames against crackers and roughnecks, usually with a few nonplayers from the other side watching from beyond the outfield, on horseback with shotguns resting on their laps.

"We knew which teams we could beat, and which ones we shouldn't," Artie explained, "because if we did we'd have a fight on our hands. With teams like that, we'd get ahead, say, 5 to 2 or so, and then get beat 6 to 5 in the late innings." But even with the nastiest teams, Artie said, the black all-stars would receive half of the gate receipts, and the take was usually pretty good.

He also told me stories about some of baseball's biggest names— things I'd never read or heard before. When Joe DiMaggio passed away, and sportswriters the world over were recalling what a great man he was, Artie related how a group of his black all-stars had visited DiMaggio's restaurant in San Francisco. They had just returned from a tour of Japan and were tired and hungry from the trip home, which had to have been grueling in the early days of overseas air travel.

After "Joltin' Joe" refused to serve them a meal, the black players quietly picked up and moved on to a restaurant down the wharf, deflated that a fellow baseball man would humiliate them just like any other racist business owner.

Artie, a person of great faith, was completely incapable of saying a negative word about another person. And so I decided to ask him about Larry Doby, the first black player in the American League, and reputed to be greatly disliked by teammates, white and black.

"Well," pondered Artie, "it's hard to believe that he and Monte Irvin (a Hall-of-Famer who might have been the first to break baseball's color barrier, were it not for his service in WWII), grew up in the same neighborhood in New Jersey."

"Why's that?" I asked.

"Because Monte Irvin is a good person," deadpanned Artie.

During our regular golf visits, Artie also inadvertently educated me about race relations in America in the '40s and '50s. He knew where he could and could not eat or shop in just about every city in the country, including mine, relating the time his roommate on the Oakland Oaks forced the race issue in a well-known downtown Portland family restaurant called "Jolly Joan's." I'd been there many times with my parents as a kid, without ever realizing they refused to serve African Americans.

The roommate, who'd virtually forced Artie to come along and refused to let him out of the booth (Wilson himself never caused a confrontation over issues of race, and would avoid them at all costs), successfully kept one table out of service for the entire evening, sitting there hours after the manager had advised, "you boys know we don't serve coloreds."

The surprising twist to Artie's story was that the ballplayer was a white guy, Billy Martin, who would later enjoy a long managerial career in the big leagues, and who had volunteered to be Wilson's roommate after Artie was told by Oakland's manager that since he was black, he'd have to room alone.

Because Artie had been elected to the Negro Leagues Hall of Fame, I felt that I was playing golf with an honest-to-goodness living legend. Occasionally on summer weekends, he'd travel to a major-league stadium somewhere to be honored with his peers. Much to Artie's surprise, in each town they visited, fans wanted autographs and speeches, and approached the old black players with a sense of awe.

And I could fully understand. Imagine, seeing and talking to a guy who actually hit against the legendary Satchel Paige! (One time, Artie told me, Paige came to pitch against the Black Barons, and the

Birmingham sportswriters had reported he was too old and couldn't pitch anymore. That made Satch mad, and when Artie started the game with a lead-off double against him, Paige stopped and yelled out to him. "You might as well sit down on second base, cause you ain't going any further." He then proceeded to strike out the next three hitters on nine pitches. Too old? Satchel Paige wouldn't get his brief shot at the majors for another four years after that.)

Artie was called up from the Pacific Coast League to join the New York Giants during the club's improbable run at the National League pennant in 1951. Used in a utility role, he wanted badly to return to the PCL, where the baseball was so good that many considered it the third major league, and where Artie was one of the most popular players, ever.

One sweltering day after we played nine holes and sat down for sodas, Artie told me how his abbreviated big league career came to an end. His manager, the fabled Leo Durocher, called Artie to his office to explain he was under heavy pressure by the team's owner to replace him with a young, hard-hitting outfielder in the Giants' farm system.

"Young Blood," said Durocher to Artie, who related that's how Durocher always addressed him, "I'm going to leave it up to you—whether you stay or go down."

"I've been telling you, that's where I want to be, back in the minors," Artie answered. "I can make as much money, and I want to play."

And so the rookie phenom, who Artie had actually mentored when both were with the Black Barons years before in Birmingham, came up to the Giants. That's how Willie Mays got to the big leagues, on Artie Wilson's say-so. (Artie has always insisted Willie's dad, "Cat" Mays, who also played with the Barons, was a far better ballplayer than his son.)

When Artie got back to his old team in Oakland and stepped to the plate for the first time, a floral arrangement paid for by the fans awaited him. The Oaks drew huge crowds for his first three home games, and he went on to enjoy a few more successful seasons in the PCL.

Artie retired in Portland after a brief stint with the Beavers in 1954. He purchased a home and went to work selling cars, but he never really quit playing baseball. He merely moved on to the "old-timer" ranks and kept having fun playing the game.

"Old-timer," by the way, is a misnomer in his case. No way does Artie look or play baseball like some old geezer, and I guess that's one of the most important things I learned from him—that things like age and race don't determine what a person can and can't do in life. Here's a guy who has been successful by all standards despite some pretty serious odds against him. Did I say that an industrial accident in Birmingham cost him a thumb along the way? It didn't seem to bother his baseball.

"I can do anything I set my mind to," he's often heard to say, "and I never failed yet."

As far as I know, Artie Wilson has never once climbed on the soap box to rail against life's injustices; he just takes the next fireballing pitcher, missed putt, or racist restaurant manager in stride. It's great to know that all of those kids at the Children's Course are learning life lessons from him, not so much by what he says, but by the type of person he is and how he's lived his life.

The last old-timers' game I saw Artie play in was a few years back at Portland's venerable Skavone Field, which had been refurbished and was celebrating its new look with the game. Former pro players from throughout the Northwest came to play, and Artie found himself hitting off a former Philadelphia Philly fastballer about half his age, a 6'6" pitcher named Wayne Twitchell.

As soon as Artie came to the plate, Twitchell noticeably increased the velocity of his pitches, from half to three-quarters speed. He also brushed Artie back with his first two pitches.

"What are you doing, Twitch?" his catcher called out, as Artie dug in.

"Hey, this is ARTIE WILSON," the pitcher answered. His third pitch was even harder and went behind Artie, who was now bearing down in full, concentrating hard on his tall rival on the mound.

The catcher called time to talk with Twitchell. "Do you realize this guy's in his eighties?" he asked.

"Do you realize this guy's ARTIE WILSON, and can still hit the ball hard?" Twitchell responded.

Pitcher and hitter smiled at one another slightly before the next pitch, giving fans the idea that this was an old, friendly rivalry, the stuff of many past old-timers' games.

The next pitch came hard down the middle, and Artie swung quick, in a short, forceful effort, not slapping the ball to left as had been his way thousands of times, but drilling it up the middle, undressing Twitchell, who fell off the mound to his left just in time to avoid taking one at about belt level.

Artie ended up on first, smiling, shaking his head and pointing at the pitcher, who grinned and actually bowed in his direction, before calling time and signaling the catcher to join him at the mound.

"I told you that was ARTIE WILSON," he said with great finality.

I looked at Artie standing on first, marveling yet again at what he could do at his age and how he had overcome this latest minor but telling challenge. I imagined him saying to himself, "That's all right."

I guess by now I've done two or three profiles of Artie, and it makes me feel good each time we put one on the news. I like to think about the thousands of people in a television audience, many of them children, who might otherwise never have heard about this good man. I'm sure that most of them, like me, have very little understanding of what all African-Americans have had to endure in the very same country we love so much. Even young men who are pursuing careers in baseball have little knowledge of the old Negro leagues or what they meant to the game.

And that's another great thing about feature reporting: by telling just one person's story, you can enlighten a great number of people. It's the power of storytelling and nothing else.

Even better for me personally is that in a rare case or two, it can lead to a lifetime friendship. I will be forever thankful that my work allowed me to get to know this sure-handed infielder and wonderful human being, Artie Wilson.

CHAPTER ELEVEN

Professional Blubbering

The difference between an optimist and a pessimist is
that a pessimist thinks things can't get much worse.
An optimist knows that they can.

—Anonymous

WHEN I STARTED WORKING as a television reporter, the standard
uniform was a suit and tie. This was also true for photographers; it
didn't matter if we were covering the police chief's press conference or
a multicar pileup on I-5, traditional business attire was the norm.

Things are different now, with nearly everyone dressing more
casually for work, but even before that trend, television reporters had
removed their coats and ties to dress more appropriately for the
weather, locale, or the type of story being covered. Today, they are
seen on the air wearing waterproof parkas in the rain, the same yellow
shirt worn by fire crews when covering forest fires and, still, the traditional coat and tie when covering city hall or the state house.

These changes make sense and are acceptable in most cases,
though I find myself wishing our reporters wouldn't appear on camera
in inclement weather wearing the hoods of their rain jackets, as they
often do. It's difficult to appear authoritative when you look like a kid
waiting for the school bus—can't they put up with a few raindrops for
the fifteen seconds they're actually on camera?

I was sensitive to such thinking as a young reporter constantly
seeking to gain credibility. While that allowed me to embrace the idea

of putting on a suit for my work, building a wardrobe wasn't cheap. I leaned heavily on the blue blazer, and took to wearing bow ties in an attempt to look older. I stopped wearing them when I decided they made me look like an idiot.

On the day we traveled to Florence for the whale story, I was wearing a favorite outfit: a forest green blazer, which I put with tan slacks, a light olive dress shirt, and a gold, green, and yellow striped tie. I topped this off with the reporter's requisite trademark, the beige trench coat, which I always had with me whether there was a hint of rain or not. I share such wardrobe detail as a preface to explaining what my clothes looked like immediately after the whale blew up. Everything was red.

For several minutes after the blast, and after the pieces of blubber stopped pelting the ground around us, a fine, red mist continued to fall. The dynamite had vaporized the whale, and initially I thought that what colored the sky, and now my clothes, was the mammal's blood. I later concluded that the tiny particles might also have been composed of small particles of blubber and whale oil. Didn't the men who hunted whales in earlier times collect several barrels of whale oil from a single kill? We were showered with it.

When I looked down at my trench coat, it was covered with a fine, red mist. I knew that my hair, hands, and face must be also coated with whale juice. Its smell was horrific, a sickening stench made up of various parts of blood and guts and death and awfulness. I felt that even if I showered and scrubbed myself clean, the ghastly stench would stay with me for a very long time.

Strangely enough, none of this sickened me or made me ill. The feeling was closer to one of loss or ruination; I'd been guilty of doing nothing more than my job when I suffered the humiliation of being so unfairly bombarded. The tendency is to take such a thing quite personally—as in, why me?—but I realized everyone around me had also been atomized pretty good. At least I had a reason, other than curiosity, for being there when it happened.

Most of the spectators, in various stages of shock and distress, were now exiting the scene, save those who wanted to get a closer look at the flattened car. Doug joined them, his sound camera now resting in its shoulder harness, to get some shots of the devastated vehicle.

I recall very little conversation during our flight back to Portland. It was as if we needed to recover from what we'd experienced; the fun-loving video death rangers, on assignment to log the next chapter in their adventurous lives, getting psychologically flattened by an ill-conceived blubber bomb.

We transferred our equipment into the Cessna, thanked the airport owner for the use of his car, and took off into the night. The horrid odor our clothes gave off filled the small cockpit of the aircraft, causing the pilot to open a small wind-wing to let in some fresh air. Prior to that, I didn't know you could open a window in a plane.

Back in Portland, we unloaded our gear and placed it in Doug's news car. That's when we received the second great jolt of the day, one which potentially could prove more devastating than the whale shrapnel which had fallen on us only hours before. Our film was missing.

"The 400-ft magazine," Doug said with urgency, "did you put it in the plane?"

"No, I don't think I did," I answered.

Doug looked stunned. We both knew that in our accepted division of labor, responsibility for the film was entirely his. I could help carry equipment, even operate a silent camera if necessary, but ultimately the shooting, transport, processing, and editing of the pictures all fell to him. I kept track of my notebook, he took care of the film.

"When did you last see the magazine?" I asked.

"In the trunk of the car," Doug said despondently. "I know I put it there. I assumed when we transferred the gear, you put it in the plane."

"So what film does that leave us?" I asked, not wanting to deflate my partner any further, but needing to know what we could broadcast in our eleven o'clock news.

"Just the prep stuff I got with the silent camera," he said, "the setup I guess is all we've got."

"And the explosion?"

"No. That would be on the missing magazine."

We drove back to the station without speaking a word to one another. There was no anger between us, but we were stinking tired and not looking forward to what was coming next.

The feeling of defeat that started in Florence increased in intensity. We might have been covered with crap before, but when we got back to the station and told the boss we didn't bring back the story, we'd really be in it deep.

Here's my brief take on the history of television news directors:

In the early days, they were more friends and colleagues of reporters than bosses; more journalists and reporters themselves than administrators. They came from radio, a few from the newspapers, and their job was to help craft the product, make a news program, and show the rest of us how it was done. They frequently covered stories themselves, often shot their own film, working side-by-side with the same reporters and cameramen they hired.

If there was a disagreement with management—over, say, how much money was spent to cover a major story—the news director would march down to the front office and fight for his guys. Sometimes he would win, sometimes he would lose, but it was always with the understanding that the reporters' immediate boss was on their side. When it came to the basic job of "getting the story," the news director was our strongest supporter, advocate, and ally.

I'm not precisely sure when that changed. There seemed to come a time in many businesses, local TV included, when the bottom line became more important than the product, as if those two could be mutually exclusive. The accountants took over, and while your basic bean counter didn't know how to make a good potato chip, he certainly knew a lot of ways to make one cheaper. The unasked question was: Would the potato chip that resulted be anything customers still wanted to eat?

The net result in local news was that audience size and ratings became more important than telling the story. The people who ran television newsrooms started talking less about what information should be shared with that evening's audience, and more about what the audience wanted to see so that it might grow larger.

As an example, it used to be that we would do series on subjects important enough to the community to warrant closer scrutiny. It might result in a three- or four-part story airing over as many nights, or perhaps a half-hour special. Both were done any time during the year.

But these new management types decreed that such series should only be produced during the four audience rating periods, or "sweeps." The subject matter also became more sensational, and even viewers came to recognize that if they were being bombarded by promos for some flashy series, it must be a rating period. Ask a young reporter in most newsrooms today to write and produce a series outside of a rating period, and he or she will be completely befuddled. Why go to all of that work if it doesn't help build up your numbers?

The other change that occurred was that the new breed of news director was more on the management team than the news team. There were exceptions, but in the main, the news director's primary task became one of keeping his department on budget and building the ratings. The real news gatherers had, in effect, lost their chief supporter and were now on their own. And heaven help the old-school reporter who still thought that reporting on the police budget or urban planning was important to the community. How would those stories help the numbers?

———

But that was of no concern to Doug and me as we returned to Channel 2 on that dark night in 1970. Pat Wilkins, the news director who had assigned us the story, was a good friend of ours. Understandably, he would be upset that we had left our film behind, and so were we, but it wouldn't be the end of the world.

Pat had stayed late to see what had become of us, and I found him in his office. He was also our main news anchor, a good-looking guy who sported a well-trimmed flattop no matter the current popular hairstyle for men; he had a deep, commanding voice, and the odd habit of wearing his belt buckle to the side, near his hip. I never knew why he did this with his belt, and I always caught myself looking at it.

"Hey, there you are," he said as he looked up from his paperwork. Then, quite obviously catching the aroma I was giving off, he suggested we step out of his office and into the newsroom to talk.

"The wires ran a pretty good story on your whale explosion," he explained. "Sounded kind of hairy—did you guys get the whole thing?"

"Well, Pat," I answered, "yes and no." Pat turned his head slightly, and this time I don't think he was reacting to the smell. He said nothing as he glanced at me, waiting for an explanation.

I told him about the explosion, about how whale blubber pounded the ground all around us, spraying us with liquid innards and forcing us to make a mad dash for our lives. I told him about the blubber smashing the car, adding for sympathy value the fact that it could have just as easily landed on us. Pat nodded, but was obviously waiting for the other shoe to drop, still saying nothing.

"The problem is we left our main magazine of film in the trunk of a car down in Florence," I finished quickly, then awaited my fate.

"Can you give us anything at all, a short story, for the eleven o'clock?" he asked, his wrinkled brow revealing growing concern.

"Not really," I said. "I mean all we have is the setup, them getting ready to blow it up. I don't think we'd look very good if we showed just that and didn't show the explosion." (Ironically, these days that's likely just what we would do. Better to "tease" it at eleven o'clock, holding the full story until the next day's main newscast following a full day of "Exploding Whale at Five" promos. The film we had in our possession would have been quite adequate for that.)

Pat looked at the floor, now deep in thought. At that point, Doug walked into the newsroom, having returned from dropping what film we did have at the processor upstairs. He came to where Pat and I were talking, which I appreciated, Doug willing to stand with me to share the heat for our screw-up. I thought for a moment that Pat might give us our second explosion of the day, but he remained calm. He looked up, first at my face, then Doug's.

"Guys," he said softly, "I don't care how you do it, but that story and those shots of that whale blowing up will be on our five o'clock news tomorrow. And I'm not renting you another damn plane." With that, he returned to his office and shortly thereafter left for home.

There was nothing for us to do but drive to Florence that night, a good four-hour trip each way. We'd be up all night.

"I'll head down there tonight," Doug offered, "it's my fault, anyway, I'll go get our film."

But I couldn't let him go alone. I was equally responsible, and Doug had to be more tired than I was, what with shooting all day long. I suggested we each go home and shower, get on some clean clothes, and meet ninety minutes later to drive back to the South Coast together. He reluctantly agreed.

My phone rang at home about forty-five minutes later.

"We're in luck," Doug said, sounding greatly relieved. "I called the guy at the airport. His son is moving to Portland and he's bringing up a load of his stuff tonight. I'm going to meet him out on I-5 at midnight to get our film. You don't need to come."

It was the best thing that had happened all day; we wouldn't have to spend a sleepless night driving to the coast. I felt much better, and a short time later, having disposed of my smelly clothes and taken a long, hot shower, I climbed wearily into bed.

As I lay there, going over the day's events and waiting for sleep to come, I could still smell that damn whale, the odor somehow permanently embedded in my nostrils. I wondered if Doug could still smell it, too, standing out on the freeway somewhere waiting for his film.

Oh well, I thought, maybe it's a small price to pay. We hadn't been killed or injured by flying whale parts, and tomorrow we'd put a story on the news that would blow everyone away.

Television reporting was all seriousness in 1970, a dead whale being treated with the same gravity as a car wreck. This reporter's goal was to look believable and to sound like David Brinkley. It was the smell, not the sun, that made me squint into the camera lens.

△ George Thornton, assistant district highway engineer, was the man in charge of the job. His bosses were off on a deer-hunting trip, leaving him to deal with much bigger game.

▽ A day at the beach was made all the more enticing when word spread in town that some state workers planned to dynamite a whale. Before the blast, escape routes weren't a consideration.

△ Until shortly before detonation, bystanders were allowed to get as close to the whale as they could stand. In the years since, I've often thought about the kid holding his nose. Not what he was doing or why he was so close to the smelly whale, but where he got that hat.

▽ Since 1970, I've heard from untold hundreds who either watched the whale blow up or had some personal connection to the incident. But my own estimate is that only fifty to seventy-five bystanders were on hand that day, and I think I ultimately outran them all.

△ I always thought this scene in our television story,
a local cop moving gawkers away from the blast area, looked like a scene from a B movie.
All of those who were moved back had to be thankful for it later.

▽ Seagulls and small scavengers were to dispose of the smaller pieces after the explosion, or so
the plan went. But after the explosion, they did what Doug and I did. They left.

△ The detonator was set up hundreds of yards into the sand dunes,
the closest anyone would be to the whale during the explosion.
Remarkably, no one was injured when the blubber came raining down.

▽ The half ton of dynamite—twenty cases of it—was brought to the scene
by a bulldozer. It was packed beneath and around the dead whale.

I've always felt that the explosion, seen from a quarter mile away, was visually unremarkable. It looks no different than those explosions we've all seen in the movies. But when one considers just *what* is being blown up—decaying blubber, bones, whale oil, and blood—it's a bit more thought-provoking.

△ The only "victim" of the exploding whale was an Oldsmobile,
parked a good quarter of a mile away. I've always considered it a strange
twist of fate that only one car in a crowded parking lot took a direct hit.

▽ I can't imagine what thoughts Walter Umenhofer must have had upon finding his
new car flattened by whale blubber. And I certainly didn't hang around to find out—
stuff was still coming down as we hightailed it out of there.

It's hard to believe that a half ton of dynamite wasn't enough
to vaporize the whale. It's even harder to believe that this ODOT worker
was able to handle the stench when he buried the remaining chunks.

CHAPTER TWELVE

Airplanes, Race Cars, and Cartoons

Every traumatic experience in our lives—every disaster, every tragedy—has within it the power to add infinitely more to our lives than it can take away.
— *"Pennypickle," a creation of David Jaquith,*
The Pennypickle Press

WHEN YOU WORK IN LOCAL television in a city the size of Portland, the twenty-third-largest market in America, the common assumption is that you're trying to make your way to a larger market or to the perceived ultimate in broadcasting, one of the big three networks.

That's never really been true for me. Having spent my entire career at only two television stations in one city, I'm what my industry refers to as a "market specific" talent. That's a nice way of saying that I look and sound so odd that no other city in America would put me on television, but I'm fine for Portland because I've done it so long that local viewers are used to me.

I actually had a station manager at KATU once tell me that she loved watching me on the news because it was "just like putting on a comfortable old pair of shoes." I'm such a sucker that I took it as a compliment. I also decided that as long as she offered me a new contract every few years, which she did, she could say what she wished.

Over the years, I have had an opportunity or two to work at the higher levels of broadcasting. There have been the occasional calls from a larger station or a headhunter, which I never took too seriously because, frankly, I didn't think I was network material. I mean, I didn't even like watching me, why would America?

Perhaps the best of these moments came when I had a chance meeting with one of the true giants in our industry. I was on a 747 flying to New York when who should walk down the aisle but Mike Wallace of CBS—he actually nodded to me as he went by, apparently stretching his legs.

I waited for him to return to his seat in first class, and then I requested that a flight attendant ask Mr. Wallace if I could speak to him for a moment. She soon returned with a pen and pad. "Mr. Wallace would like to know what you want to talk to him about," she advised.

That was some of the hardest writing I've ever had to do. How does a reporter write a few, brief sentences compelling enough to win the interest of one of the most heralded reporters in the history of our profession? I can't recall what I wrote, probably something inane about me being in the business too, blah blah.

But the next thing I know, someone in the aisle is putting a hand almost directly in my face. As I look up, the person says, "How do you do, I'm Mike Wallace." He'd come back from first class to my seat to find me, and I found myself momentarily speechless as I shook his hand. I had interviewed enough big-name celebrities by then that I should not have been thrown off by meeting one, but I was.

At Mr. Wallace's suggestion, we found a row of empty seats in the middle section of the aircraft, sat down, and drank Scotch and smoked cigarettes and talked for the two hours we had left before landing at JFK. Okay, they were my cigarettes, and I was buying the Scotch, but I would have paid a much higher price than that to pick this man's brain about our business and career directions.

His insight was priceless, and it was easy to see what made him a good interviewer. At one point, I recall his aggressively questioning me about my future plans.

"You know what your problem is, young man?" he charged. "You don't actually know what you want to do. You've never really thought it through—where you want to go next and down the road. You really don't know, do you?"

I'm normally pretty laid back, but this made me want to jump down his throat with an answer. Damn straight I knew what I wanted to do, and he could just shut up while I told him. That was my thought before realizing I had fallen prey to Mike Wallace's interview style—it's what caused all of those reluctant story subjects to eagerly tell their side of the story.

We had a wonderful conversation and before we parted, Mr. Wallace stood up in the aisle, and had a final word for me.

"I think you might have what it takes," he said, "and CBS pays me a lot of money because I have such good judgment. I'll have someone call you when you get back to Portland—you should work for us. My son Chris is at our O&O in Chicago; that might be a good place for you." O&O is an industry term used to describe those television stations in the biggest markets that are *owned and operated* by the networks, in this case, CBS.

I was floored. I was also very drunk at this point, but I guarantee that's what he said, and I couldn't believe my ears.

True to his word, Mr. Wallace later put me in touch with two CBS executives, Lane Vernardos, news director at WBBM-TV in Chicago, and Robert Wustler, the station manager who would later become president of the network. Their attitude seemed to be, we talked to Mike, when can you come to work?

My attitude was, tomorrow.

At that time, my wife, Vicki, and I had two sons, and we were about to leave on a camping trip to the high desert of Central Oregon. On our first night we'd just put our little boys to sleep in the tent, and we were sitting by a campfire, relaxing with a glass of wine. The stars were brilliant in an unbelievably clear sky above; the night was perfect, without so much as a breath of wind. Life was good. Would this be a good time to talk about moving to Chicago?

Turned out we didn't have to talk about it at all. We both loved our native state and knew there couldn't be a better place to raise our children. Our home in Portland was ninety minutes from the mountains, the sea, or the desert; we had forests in our own neighborhood. The prospect of a job in a bigger market, other than perhaps fueling my professional ego, didn't seem as appealing as it had when I was drinking Scotch with Mike Wallace on the plane several days before.

Also, what if I went to Chicago and failed, the viewers thinking I looked like an old shoe, and not necessarily a comfortable one at that?

I sent Mr. Wallace a thank-you note, called Mr. Vernardos with my thanks and regrets, and put away my network dreams forever. There would be other inquiries in the future, none taken very seriously. In the coming years, I would work with many reporters who went on to jobs at the network level, some of them returning to Portland, having also decided that the livability of a place can be more important than career advancement.

I haven't had any regrets about that decision made many years ago. As a feature reporter, I've met and reported on so many incredible people I would have never known had I taken a job reporting for a major network. In fact, networks have very few people on their staffs assigned to cover the "lights and brights," the fluff, the good news. It's what I love.

And of all the different types of feature subjects, my favorites are those people who overcome extreme physical challenges to achieve their goals in life. Because I tend to be a complainer who secretly feels the entire world plots to keep me from reaching mine, I have an admiration for those who take even the largest obstacles in stride without so much as a whimper. I've met dozens of these blissfully ignorant achievers, but a couple of them are at the top of my all-time inspirational list. Both take facing "extreme physical challenges" to an entirely new level because, for all practical purposes, neither of these guys have, well, bodies.

———————

When I met Doc Lavender at his home in Keizer, a small Willamette Valley community about forty minutes south of Portland, he was tossing a ball for his mangy dog. His backyard wasn't much to look at either, with overgrown grass, and various rusting cans and car parts scattered about.

Doc looked like a head sitting on a wheelchair. Short, toothpick arms did emerge from somewhere near the seat, and one of his deformed hands would kind of flip a tennis ball Frisbee-like in the dog's direction. Because he could only move his hand several inches, Doc would try to use whatever body he had to give his toss enough momentum to actually reach the dog. It was hard to watch, Doc nearly falling out of the chair with the inertia of each throw.

Doyle "Doc" Lavender had been in a wheelchair since the age of three, his body ravaged by rheumatoid arthritis. But that hadn't kept him from dreaming big dreams. He wanted to be a professional race car driver.

"At five years old," he told me, "my goal was to set the land speed record with a gasoline-powered automobile."

He appeared to be in his forties. He wore a lavender baseball cap and tank top of the same color, sported a pierced ear, tinted glasses, and a sparse goatee. When he spoke, he leaned his head back into the backrest of his mobilized wheelchair, but his voice was deep and full of confidence. His words came in well-measured sentences, like a man who knew his thoughts well and shared them with great certainty.

There were skeptics years before when he bought a completely trashed 1935 Nash, which was being used at the time as a chicken coop on a farm not far from Doc's home.

"Most everybody said, 'Yeah, right dude, sure it will be a race car,'" Doc recalled during the interview for our story.

But seven months later, and with the help of many friends who wanted to see Doc realize his dream, he had a beautiful race car, well prepared for the drag strip. It was painted lavender, of course, and dubbed by Doc "The Disabled Chicken Coop," the words written beautifully in professional pinstriping on both doors. Doc took his car racing, and it turned out he was a pretty good driver. The only assistance he required was being lifted from his chair to the driver's seat, which his companion, Judy Hinkleman, rendered quite effortlessly since Doc appeared to weigh considerably less than a hundred pounds.

We watched him race on a Sunday afternoon at the Woodburn drag strip, south of Portland. My photographer, Mike Slowik (a great shooter and editor, who I did hundreds of stories with), rode in the car and shot Doc during his quarter-mile run. It resulted in exciting video, the revved-up engine giving off a tremendous racket, Doc with his head leaning back in the seat, working hand throttle and steering wheel with one hand, the gear shift with another. I've watched that video several times and still don't know how he did it—this was a guy who couldn't answer the phone without using a metal rod with a hook on the end of it.

On the day we watched him race, Doc Lavender finished third out of thirty-two cars in his class. He was pleased with that, but told us his racing involved much more than the need for speed or competition. He had a point to prove and wanted everyone in the grandstands to know about it.

"My favorite saying," he explained, "is that I'm proving the ability in disability. And to me, if you drop the *dis*, it's *ability*. If I can do it in my situation, anybody can."

He paused, then tapped his heart. "But it has to be in here. You have to have it inside."

Within two years of his first race, Doc Lavender was winning pro events, the fastest driver in fields of thirty-three or more. Longtime drag race fans were amazed to watch Judy lift him into the car for each run, then watch him burn up the track. Doc told me he once estimated that in a year of racing, mainly on California drag strips, he'd been seen by a quarter of a million people. His hope was that they would view him, and others with physical challenges, with new eyes.

"I hope they see me as a competitor," he said, "and as another person who, if given half a chance, will whip you. I think I can help them start to realize that people with disabilities are just that—people. That's the bottom line."

Doc died of a brain aneurysm in the summer of 1997. Judy Hinkleman donated his beautiful lavender race car to the National Hot Rod Association Museum in Pomona, California, where it resides today, Doc's message living on.

I've thought and wondered about Doc Lavender often. What was it that allowed him to overlook such huge barriers and succeed, while other people, like me, are thrown into fits of despair by the smallest of difficulties? Part of it had to be that heart thing—having it inside, as Doc demonstrated. But I also think it might have had something to do with what he said his dad taught him, back when he was a little boy dreaming about setting that land speed record.

"Dad told me that I could do anything I wanted," he said. "I just had to figure out how."

Because Doc believed him, he proved it true. He never did set that land speed record, but a winning attitude allowed him to get just where he wanted to go, and fast!

———

A few times each year I receive a newsletter in the mail called *The Pennypickle Press.* I always take time to study the envelope it arrives in. My name and address fill nearly the entire front of the envelope, the words beautifully written in oversized script, the loops of the letters so large that they've been filled in with colored pencils. There's usually a cartoon to the left side, a bird wearing a business suit and hat, sitting on a branch with musical notes all around, also colored in greens and purples and reds. Someone has gone to a great deal of work just on the envelope.

The Pennypickle Press is the work of David Jaquith and his wife, Mary, who live in the rural community of Lafayette, Oregon. David also used to write a column for the weekly *Newburg Graphic*. But I am certain that his real work in life, and what he loves to create most, is the newsletter.

Each issue is a compendium of positive thinking, hopeful advice, and thought-provoking musings, all of which come solely from the minds and pens of David and Mary. They share their insight, most of it faith-based, through stories and poetry, humorous definitions, sayings, drawings, and regularly appearing cartoon characters such as Clancy Clump, Jonathan Quill, Andy McGumph, and Pennypickle himself.

Every newsletter also contains a box explaining precisely what the publication stands for, as a newspaper masthead might, though the explanation changes each time. One such banner reads:

"*The Pennypickle Press*—moving past analyzing life to experiencing it to the full, trusting that in doing so, all obligations will be met, and the divine virus of love will spread without coercion or making anyone feel guilty."

And another:

"*The Pennypickle Press*—issued free for fun and profit. Mailed with consistently intermittent spasmodicity. Progeny of David and Mary Jaquith, who, like you, keep busy sifting the wheat from the chaff."

It's impossible for a reader not to be amused, uplifted, and encouraged by the newsletter, which David and Mary have been publishing since the 1970s. But what their readers might never learn from its pages is that for more than twenty years, David has been flat on his back.

The man is completely bedridden by rheumatoid arthritis, and does all of the writing by computer from a hospital bed set up in the living room of the couple's apartment. He also does all of the cartooning, having had his gnarled fingers surgically implanted with wires so that he can write and draw.

I have never met anyone with a more positive outlook than David Jaquith, nor have I ever met anyone more justified in being completely ticked off about what life has dealt him. But he steadfastly refuses to be a victim, and insists he's not an invalid.

"We all have limitations that we work in," he told me when I interviewed him for our television series. "The idea is to find out what your limitations are and be creative in that context."

David was in his midsixties when we met, had thin silver hair, and wore black, horn-rimmed glasses. He spoke in soft tones, carefully selecting his words. Mary sat nearby, and it was evident that the two are completely devoted to one another. She is his full-time caregiver, and they have an incredible partnership.

David wrote about their division of labor in the newsletter:

"I have played the role of chief word compounder, Mary the supportive role.

"It works out that way because first, compounding words comes easier for El Verboso; secondly, I have the only computer in the house.

"She takes the pages off the computer printer, runs them through the copier, collates, staples, folds, stuffs, stamps. She buys the paper and toner, and hand colors my drawings on the envelopes. She reboots my touchy computer when it shuts down in midsentence, and for years she'd pick bits of paper out of the printer roller with tweezers when it jammed.

"All this Mary does, plus running the house, car, and me . . . Something I am acutely conscious of, as I'm not much help.

"What appears on these pages is but a hint of our lifework, which is, as we often say here, to go on record, to give family and friends a glimpse of our intentions. We have room to mature, you'll note."

David and Mary also seem to have an ongoing discussion on *everything*, plenty of give and take, which is often reported on in their newsletter. As in this exchange:

"Out of the blue, Mary asks: 'If you are *inert* when lying still, are you *ert* when you are doing something?' Before I could answer, she had another one: 'If you are not interested, are you *terested*?' And you thought you had problems."

———————

Here are some other examples of the Jaquith musings, gleaned from their newsletters:

"On rating the gift of life: Cherish each of your moments, for they are precious to heaven beyond your dreams. In them lie all the marvels of eternal creation, mercifully scaled to your capacity to experience them."

A cartoon which shows an angry-looking clergyman looking toward the heavens: "Don't make me come up there!" with a further line of explanation at the bottom of the panel, "Rev. Brewster, displeased (again) with God for causing problems in his congregation."

"Listening with half an ear, I heard someone on CNN speak of 'separating those who quietly know from those who desperately hope.' It got my attention. I jotted it down and later, it transmorphed itself into a prayer: Let those of us who quietly know reach out to those of us who desperately hope, and explore together the wonders and the mysteries of life."

"All you need is love . . . and a little common sense. If you'll forgive the contradiction."

"Reading about the giant star cloud, Antares, I said to Mary: 'A guy here says you can pack 400 million of our suns inside Antares and have room to wiggle.' Mary, (busy untangling yarn): 'Why would anyone want to do that?' Me: 'Do what, pack a bunch of suns in Antares or wiggle?' By then she had disappeared into the kitchen, leaving the matter, well, up in the air."

"What are acts of terrorism but anger and resentment, such as mine, cherished to the extreme, and acted out?" (—from Mary's notes jotted on a small piece of paper and tucked into a book.)

"The Pennypickle Press—a journey shared. Peace is not just the absence of war. It is people with a change of heart."

In addition to the newsletter and his regular column, David (also with Mary's help) has written and illustrated three books. But, remarkably, when we talked about all he has accomplished despite not even being able to leave his bed, David said he felt guilty about it.

"Because other people who can do a lot more," he explained, "aren't necessarily as complete, or feel as complete as I do, about their lives."

I discovered that David and Mary Jaquith absolutely believe in a philosophy that their make-believe friend, Pennypickle, has espoused often for their readers: every disaster can add rather than take away from life. They're living proof that everyone, no matter what dreadful circumstances life has brought, can indeed make their own contributions and share something of value with others.

"Life does provide that," David told me. "It's just a matter of getting the stuff out of the way that keeps it from happening."

During our visit, I watched Mary take care of David's various needs. I thought about what tension and turmoil one person's total dependence on another might potentially bring, but I saw nothing but mutual respect and kindness between the two. What's more, they sincerely enjoyed each other. The gentle chiding, the wordplay and intellectual give and take, the friendly teasing—all of it somehow part of the fabric of their daily routine—told me that here were two people who deeply cared for one another. The incredibly limiting circumstances of David's physical condition, because of how they dealt with it together, meant little.

The television story I did on the Jaquiths focused on their newsletter and the fact that such an uplifting and inspiring publication was the creation of a man who had every right to hate life and everything about it. It was a story about overcoming physical limitations. But more than anything else, I decided, it was a love story.

We need more of those on the evening news.

CHAPTER THIRTEEN

How It All Began

I read the news today, oh boy . . .
—*The Beatles*, from "A Day in the Life,"
Lennon/McCartney, 1967

HERE'S MY TAKE on the history of television news:

It started in the 1950s and was like radio with pictures. At first, since most of the early practitioners were radio guys, the pictures didn't matter much. A guy sitting at a desk in front of a funny looking microphone, reading from some papers he held in his hands, was the television news. Sometimes this guy even smoked while doing the news, maybe because that's what they did in radio.

Then someone decided that, since this was television, there should be more to look at. So they started shooting film and putting it on the news. It didn't matter much what—they shot a lot of meetings and other guys just talking—but since the audience really hadn't seen these things before in moving pictures, that was okay.

The next thing that happened was some television newspeople figured out that the cooler the pictures—like car wrecks and fires instead of just meetings and talking guys—the more the audience seemed to like it. This presented a slight conflict because most often the coolest pictures, say, of dog shows and beauty pageants, came from the least important stories. So for quite awhile, television news tried to do both, combining some neat things to look at, and some important things to know about but not much fun to see. That meant stories about boring city council and school board meetings, but also some good "visuals" as they came to be called, cops arresting bad guys, and beauty shots of Mt. Hood and Rose Festival floats.

Oh, I forgot to say that underlying all of this was a major problem encountered by the first TV newspeople—they didn't have very much time to work with. A half-hour newscast, for instance, would only contain about as much information as approximately two columns of the newspaper. Take away time for sports, weather, and commercials, and the "news hole" wasn't very large at all.

But no problem, said the broadcasting pioneers, because we're not supposed to be the newspaper anyway; we're supposed to be like news on the radio, actually a headline service, but with pictures. If people want more detailed information, they're going to have to get it where they always have—from the newspapers and magazines. We'll just do things in brief, to give everyone an idea of what's going on.

Very few of those early TV news types cared much about how good the writing was in their stories. This was because very few newspaper people—who did care how good the writing was—crossed over into television news. They mostly stayed right where they were, and began hating people in television news for becoming local celebrities, even though they couldn't write, which was what journalism was supposed to be about.

Next, a really frightening thing happened to the TV people, I think in about the mid-1960s. They had begun doing research that told them how to do the news better, or in other words, how to make an audience grow by giving viewers what they wanted to see. But surprisingly, the research showed that most people were getting most of their information from television news, not from the newspapers and magazines like they were supposed to. This was not good since TV had only enough time to be a headline service, and people needed much more information than that.

The television people decided they had to do more. Newscasts were lengthened from thirty to sixty minutes, and the evening news "block" was expanded to include an additional thirty minutes of national news provided by the networks.

What's more, television now tried to cover *everything*, just like the newspapers. Reporters were assigned beats, such as the legislature or the state board of higher education; news promotion campaigns started promising viewers that if they watched Channel X, they would get "all of the news." Of course, there was still the need for attention-getting pictures, and there had to be time for sports, weather, and the commercials, all crammed into space the equivalent of (now) four newspaper columns.

Up to this point, it hadn't really mattered what people on the news looked like—whoever came over from radio to get this industry going was fine. But now, with the help of all that research, news directors decided that attractive people, hopefully with authoritative, though not necessarily conversational, voices, might make the newscast even more appealing to viewers. This began the era of the suave, handsome, and heavily hair-sprayed anchorman, which upset the newspaper people even more.

It followed, then, that the first women came on board, but they were never given important stories to cover, only flower shows and fashion stuff. And they were never, ever allowed to be news "anchors," the people who sat at the desk with papers and talked. It was Huntley and Brinkley and Walter Cronkite and maybe, in a few strange places, a weather girl or two, but forget about women doing anything else.

There was one other thing that happened along the way. Someone discovered if you scared people a little bit with a television news story, like if there were some very alarming pictures to go with it, viewers liked that. This resulted in a lot of newscasts starting with serious crime stories, the underlying message being that this just might happen to you, Mr. and Mrs. Viewer. That still goes on today, and even people who don't work in television news know to say, "If it bleeds, it leads."

In later years, TV newscasts would lighten up some, the anchor people (who would also later include women) actually being instructed for a time to engage in "happy talk," so viewers would think they were somehow normal and not news robots. But in these early days, the evening news was as serious as, well, a newspaper, and only with a very few seconds at the end allotted for lighter subjects during the final, or "kicker," story.

This kicker might involve pictures of a polar bear at the zoo playing with a ball in his swimming pool, for instance, the purpose of the last story being to show people that even though they had just seen a lot of bad news, things were still okay at the zoo and various places, so they should watch again tomorrow, to see both what bad things could happen to them and also that things were really just fine.

———————

When Doug Brazil and I came upon the scene in the late 1960s, the serious news thing was still going on. Our main newscasters rarely smiled or laughed—this was good, because it made them seem more like real newspeople, the ones still at the newspapers who had no need at all to look suave or hair-sprayed, let alone happy.

I don't remember any funny stories being done at all back then, except the "Two-Headed Dog" spoof story we did as an experiment. Well, there was also the Ken Kesey drug initiative story, which Doug and I thought was funny, but no one else got it.

Given that backdrop, imagine the dilemma we faced when asked to cover a story about some state workers who packed twenty cases of dynamite under a dead whale and pushed the plunger, showering everyone with blood and blubber and flattening some guy's brand-new car.

How would you write it? Is it a humorous story with a serious twist, or a serious story that suddenly went wrong, leading to humorous results? At first, I honestly didn't know which way to go.

The story's elements were obvious; we had pictures of the disposal preparation, a couple of sound bites from the official in charge, the explosion itself, and its aftermath, scenes of smelly eyewitnesses and the smashed, odorous Oldsmobile. Putting them together chronologically made sense, but what was the attitude of our story?

The very idea of exploding a whale was odd, and the result—a whale-meat shower that made everyone nauseous but didn't cause a single injury—was, well, funny. On the other hand, it might be considered lead-story serious. Was it more akin to the "here's the bad stuff that happened today" stories that began every newscast, or closer to the "polar bear playing with his ball" stories which ended them? The truth is I'm still not sure.

But there were a couple of factors that determined our direction. First, we knew our story would evoke a response from viewers no matter what; the writing would not make or break the story.

Prior to airing it, we had run the film of the explosion and the flattened car on a newsroom projector enough times to know that these scenes elicited a spirited response from even the most veteran of our reporters, guys who'd seen just about everything. There were shouts and laughter and great hilarity each time someone else would see it for the first time. We could therefore comfortably take the television reporter's fallback position: let the pictures tell the story; the story's "direction" was nearly a nonissue.

The second influence was strictly personal. I was a twenty-three-year-old reporter trying to make it in a medium where all of the other reporters were in at least their thirties and forties. I had previously been denied the opportunity to be the station's legislative reporter because the news director said I looked too young, that no one would pay attention to "some kid reporting from the state capitol." So whenever I appeared on camera, I did my best to look and sound older—authoritative and sure of myself. This was my idiotic bow-tie period.

The exploding whale story, I finally decided, would be written and delivered more seriously than humorously. There may be room for a little fun—a play on words here, an alliteration there—but we had best report it straight and let the explosion be the big payoff. Indeed, the story didn't need to raise serious questions about what the State Highway Division people had done, or the soundness of their plan, because our film would raise questions enough on its own.

The story first aired on our five o'clock newscast of November 13, 1970. While I can't recall precisely what was written to introduce this prerecorded package, or the "tag" which may have followed it with concluding information, what follows is the script as I wrote it.

TAKE SOF (Sound on Film):

LINNMAN/STANDUP: "IT HAD TO BE SAID . . . THE OREGON STATE HIGHWAY DIVISION NOT ONLY HAD A WHALE OF A PROBLEM ON ITS HANDS, IT HAD A STINKING WHALE OF A PROBLEM: WHAT TO DO WITH ONE FORTY-FIVE-FOOT, EIGHT-TON WHALE, DEAD ON ARRIVAL ON A BEACH NEAR FLORENCE." (RUNS: 15)

TAKE SF (SILENT FILM) VOICE OVER:

IT HAD BEEN SO LONG SINCE A WHALE HAD WASHED UP IN LANE COUNTY, NOBODY COULD REMEMBER HOW TO GET RID OF ONE.

IN SELECTING ITS BATTLE PLAN, THE HIGHWAY DIVISION DECIDED IT COULDN'T BE BURIED BECAUSE IT MIGHT SOON BE UNCOVERED, IT COULDN'T BE CUT UP AND THEN BURIED BECAUSE NOBODY WANTED TO CUT IT UP, AND IT COULDN'T BE BURNED. SO DYNAMITE IT WAS, SOME 20 CASES, OR, A HALF TON OF IT.

THE HOPE WAS THAT THE LONG DEAD PACIFIC GRAY WHALE WOULD BE ALMOST DISINTEGRATED BY THE BLAST, AND THAT ANY SMALL PIECES STILL AROUND AFTER THE EXPLOSION WOULD BE TAKEN CARE OF BY SEAGULLS AND OTHER SCAVENGERS. INDEED, THE SEAGULLS HAD BEEN STANDING NEARBY ALL DAY.

AS EVERYTHING WAS BEING MADE READY, WE ASKED GEORGE THORNTON, THE HIGHWAY ENGINEER IN CHARGE OF THE PROJECT, FOR HIS FINAL OBSERVATION.

TAKE SOF: (Sound on film)

GEORGE THORNTON, STATE HIGHWAY ENGINEER: "WELL, I'M CONFIDENT THAT IT WILL WORK. THE ONLY THING IS WE'RE

NOT SURE JUST EXACTLY HOW MUCH EXPLOSIVES IT WILL TAKE
TO DISINTEGRATE THIS THING SO THE SCAVENGERS, SEAGULLS,
CRABS AND WHAT NOT, CAN CLEAN IT UP."

LINNMAN: "IS THERE ANY CHANCE IT MIGHT BE MORE THAN A
ONE DAY JOB?"

THORNTON: "UH, IF THERE'S ANY LARGE CHUNKS LEFT, AND
UH, WE MAY HAVE SOME OTHER CLEAN UP. POSSIBLY SET
ANOTHER CHARGE." (RUNS: 24)

TAKE SF/VO:

THE DYNAMITE WAS BURIED PRIMARILY ON THE LEEWARD SIDE
OF THE BIG MAMMAL SO THAT MOST OF THE REMAINS WOULD
BE BLOWN TOWARD THE SEA.

ABOUT SEVENTY-FIVE BYSTANDERS, MOST OF THEM RESIDENTS
WHO HAD FIRST FOUND THE WHALE TO BE AN OBJECT OF CURIOSITY
BEFORE THEY TIRED OF ITS SMELL, WERE MOVED BACK A QUARTER OF A
MILE AWAY.

THE SAND DUNES THERE WERE COVERED WITH SPECTATORS
AND LANDLUBBER NEWSMEN, SOON TO BECOME LANDBLUBBER
NEWSMEN. FOR THE BLAST BLASTED BLUBBER BEYOND ALL
BELIEVABLE BOUNDS.

TAKE NAT SOF: (COUNTDOWN & EXPLOSION) (RUNS: 28)

TAKE SF:

OUR CAMERAS STOPPED ROLLING IMMEDIATELY AFTER THE
BLAST. THE HUMOR OF THE ENTIRE SITUATION SUDDENLY GAVE
WAY TO A RUN FOR SURVIVAL, AS HUGE CHUNKS OF WHALE
BLUBBER FELL EVERYWHERE.

PIECES OF MEAT PASSED HIGH OVER OUR HEADS WHILE
OTHERS WERE FALLING AT OUR FEET. THE DUNES WERE RAPIDLY
EVACUATED AS SPECTATORS ESCAPED BOTH THE FALLING DEBRIS
AND THE OVERWHELMING SMELL.

A PARKED CAR OVER A QUARTER MILE FROM THE BLAST SITE WAS THE TARGET OF ONE LARGE CHUNK—THE PASSENGER COMPARTMENT, LITERALLY SMASHED.

FORTUNATELY, NO HUMAN WAS HIT AS BADLY AS THE CAR; HOWEVER, EVERYONE AT THE SCENE WAS COVERED WITH SMALL PARTICLES OF DEAD WHALE.

AS FOR THE SUCCESS OF THE EFFORT, THE SEAGULLS WHO WERE SUPPOSED TO CLEAN THINGS UP WERE NOWHERE IN SIGHT, EITHER SCARED AWAY BY THE EXPLOSION OR KEPT AWAY BY THE SMELL. THAT DIDN'T REALLY MATTER, THE REMAINING CHUNKS WERE OF SUCH A SIZE THAT NO RESPECTABLE SEAGULL WOULD ATTEMPT TO TACKLE ANYWAY.

AS DARKNESS BEGAN TO SET IN, THE HIGHWAY CREWS WERE BACK ON THE BEACH BURYING THE REMAINS, INCLUDING A LARGE PIECE OF CARCASS WHICH NEVER LEFT THE BLAST SITE.

IT MIGHT BE CONCLUDED THAT SHOULD A WHALE EVER WASH ASHORE IN LANE COUNTY AGAIN, THOSE IN CHARGE WILL NOT ONLY REMEMBER WHAT TO DO, THEY'LL CERTAINLY REMEMBER WHAT NOT TO DO.

(TOTAL LENGTH: 3:25)

–30–

The story is not at all what I would write today. It is long, its sentences awkward and cumbersome. Television news has never bothered much with rewrite—at best, a producer may look over a script and revise it slightly before giving it approval—but this story cries for revision. It's wordy and labors to reach its conclusions.

It also contains an inaccuracy or two. I had the type of whale wrong, of course, but can't imagine today why I would write such misleading sentences as, "Our cameras stopped rolling immediately after the blast," implying they had somehow been knocked out of action. In reality, they stopped because Doug and I stopped them, which would have been necessary before we both started running for our lives.

Also, I dearly wish I hadn't written what I must have thought at the time was a clever, alliterative sentence, "The blast blasted blubber beyond all believable bounds." Innumerable times in the years since, my four sons—back when they were young boys and now as grown men—have recited those words to me completely out of the blue and without provocation. They use the same David Brinkley impersonation I was guilty of affecting on the original story track, and seem to like to do it for no other reason I can think of than to dog me. And it works every time.

Finally, in retrospect, each time I see or read the story—and it's been hundreds of times—I am dismayed to realize how short it is on content following the explosion.

How could we not have interviewed others on the scene to get their reactions to nearly being killed by flying blubber? Why did we not talk to Walter Umenhofer about how it felt to get his new Oldsmobile wiped out in such a bizarre way? How could we not have caught up with George Thornton once again for his reaction to what had happened? (Not sure how much explosive to use, eh George? Well, just what was that, too much or not enough?)

In retrospect, all I can conclude is that we must have been completely driven by the desire to get our film back to town and on the news that night. There can be no other reason to leave such an incredible scene and bizarre story without all of the necessary parts needed for a more complete story. Thankfully, and I think mainly because the explosion itself is just plain fun to watch, other writers and media critics haven't been too hard on our story.

"This is a broadcast classic," wrote Don Fitzpatrick in his long-running, online ShopTalk newsletter. "The piece is well written and holds up well over twenty years later." Well, I'm not sure it holds up thirty years later, but I appreciate Mr. Fitzpatrick's review.

And I know one part of the story was absolutely perfect—Doug Brazil's film of the event. A reporter's nightmare is to get back to the shop and discover the pictures needed to tell a story are not all there, that the photographer has somehow failed to shoot some key element.

It was quite clear, (once we had finally retrieved our film from Florence!) that Doug had captured it all, from start to finish.

Also, before we completed our story for broadcast, he even found a way to superimpose a countdown over the film to signal the start of the explosion. It added greatly to the drama of our story just before the blast; all is quiet over a long, static shot of the whale as the numbers appear and begin the countdown, 10–9–8, etc. I've watched live audiences view the story, and invariably shouts such as "Oh, no!" and "Yes!" pick up in anticipation as the numbers start to click off.

The story was broadcast once only in its original form during our five o'clock news. In order to incorporate Doug's countdown, it was preproduced for playback on videotape. However, our original film was reedited by others for a shorter story, which aired on the late news at eleven o'clock; the film outtakes were most likely tossed in the trash.

By the next working day, Doug and I had moved on to other assignments, the whale having become yesterday's news. Other than the appreciative comments of coworkers and congratulations for having placed the story on Sunday's network news, the subject was no longer of much interest to us. We knew that our original report on the exploding whale, good or bad, would never be seen again.

CHAPTER FOURTEEN

Really Playing It as It Lies

Don't hurry, don't worry. You're only here for a short visit.
So be sure to smell the flowers along the way.
—Walter Hagen

THE PEOPLE WHO have the best deal by far in television, in terms of ease of work, good pay, perquisites, recognition, you name it, are the news anchors and talk show hosts. Those just happen to be the two jobs I've done in local TV for the better part of the last thirty-six years. I didn't plan it and can't explain how it happened, but I'm eternally grateful for it.

Name anyone working in local TV, the writers and producers who actually piece together the newscasts—people who routinely work an eight-hour shift or more without even leaving a noisy newsroom for lunch—the directors, technical people, and engineers who get the newscast, somehow, into people's television sets at home, the photographers who daily risk life and limb to get "the shots," the video editors, graphics designers, sales people, accountants, secretaries, receptionists, and virtually everyone else who isn't "on the air," all of these people work harder and longer than your basic anchor. And they do it for less money and little recognition.

Most anchors in large markets don't cover stories like reporters do, and few of them write anything at all. Some rewrite, mainly to improve poor copy so they don't look like donkeys on the air, but the majority of them simply hang around getting ready for the next newscast, tending to their makeup and other important things. (My fellow anchors who might read this will object mightily, but they know it's true, except in small markets where anchors may also report, sell ads, wash the news cars, whatever. But this is only so much dues-paying, which must be done for awhile before you're qualified to hang around and do nothing.)

There are, however, some exceptions, and in the years that I've read the news and hosted magazine or talk shows, I've also chosen to write and produce stories. There are a couple of reasons for this, neither of which have to do with an innate love of work or some saintly disposition which makes me want to share the load with my brother and sister reporters. I just like storytelling, and with a nightly audience in the thousands, why wouldn't a broadcast journalist want to seek out and share the best stories in his or her community? Besides, putting on my makeup doesn't take that much time—just trowel in the cracks and I'm ready to go.

Also, back in 1988, I was given added incentive to report on good people who you rarely see on the news.

The afternoon talk show I had returned to Channel 2 to do, creatively named *Two at Four*—a program as exciting as its time period—had just been cancelled. Our programmers had routinely picked up as many syndicated talk shows as possible and aired them in off-hours, this to prevent competing stations from getting them and counter-programming against our locally produced talk shows.

But someone on our staff bought a new show that cost too much to bury—$15,000 per daily episode—and so it was given my afternoon slot. The program was called *Oprah*, and while none of us had ever heard of it or its host, the practice of purchasing syndicated shows to protect ours ironically had done us in. At the station's request, and because there was time left on my contract, I went back to anchoring the nightly news and waited for the inevitable. I knew it wouldn't be long before the bad news started to overwhelm me and drive me out of the business once again.

However, at about the same time, my bosses asked me to produce twenty feature stories on unknown local people who were doing remarkable things. They would be packaged, along with original music, graphics, and the series' own promos, and shown nightly over a month's period to springboard a broader station identification campaign. The consultant that sold us this series concept, called *The Spirit of the Northwest*, guaranteed that Channel 2 would soon be known far and wide as the "Spirit" station, and darned if it wasn't. I did the twenty stories about people who had "the spirit," whatever that was, and Channel 2's visibility in the community increased in measurable ways.

The first piece was a profile of a Southern Oregon sawmill owner who, seeing the end of his business and the wood products industry in our state, paid for his soon-to-be-laid-off workers to be retrained as computer programmers. After I'd done such a story every weeknight for a month, however, I asked my bosses if I could keep doing them— I was having a blast. Meeting these remarkable people and telling their stories seemed to be the antidote to my nightly reading of the doom and gloom news. Sure, there's a lot of terrible stuff happening, was my attitude, but before we say good night, you got to see this!

Our series led us to a crusty yet likeable retiree who set up a collection network for gathering beer and soda pop can pull tabs, which could be recycled. Lloyd White, "The Pull Tab King," recruited his fellow Masons, retirees, truckers, school teachers, students, and others throughout the Western United States to collect thousands of dollars worth of salvageable aluminum each year. Proceeds from its sale were used to pay for lifesaving kidney transplants for those who couldn't afford them.

We met a lovely, talented, ninety-year-old jazz singer, Celia Davis, who still performed nightly in smoky clubs to the delight of her fans; a Vietnam veteran who labored full-time planting vegetable gardens, without charge, for needy seniors; and a mother who started an ambulance service in her town after her own son died for a lack of emergency care.

My photographer and I followed a police horse too spooked to work the streets anymore, but still perfectly capable of giving disabled kids their first horseback ride, and a guy with Parkinson's disease who had walked across America and back, or at least the equivalent distance, on his treadmill.

We covered groups, too, one arranging adoptions for retired racing greyhounds, saving the dogs from becoming dog food themselves; another, running a summer camp for kids with cancer who might not otherwise in their too-brief lives experience a campfire or catch a fish. All of these people were unpaid and didn't receive government handouts, but unanimously felt they were benefiting more from their efforts than the people they served.

We encountered runners who completed full marathons, despite life-threatening illnesses or disabilities, blind cabinetmakers who nonetheless crafted beautiful work, and downtown businesspeople who started an employment and education program designed to rescue the very street kids who hassled them for spare change every day.

Before I knew it, the month of "good news" stories I had been asked to do had extended to twelve years, and the twenty stories had grown to 1,215 feature profiles. Research may show that news audiences won't watch a steady diet of good news, but I knew that my viewers, to oversimplify just a bit, were getting the good along with the bad. Further, as I explained to those news directors who didn't like feature stories, if we're covering gang or drug problems in our community, shouldn't we also check in on the problem solvers who are trying to keep kids out of gangs or off drugs?

Most of my bosses and, more importantly, the management of Channel 2, tended to agree. You don't see one-thousand-part series on the news anywhere, certainly none devoted to subjects that might be uplifting and, at times, inspirational. I'm pleased that my television station let me do it.

Even so, I did notice over time that while the *Spirit of the Northwest* series helped elevate our newscast to number one in the ratings year after year, the viewers I personally encountered rarely if ever asked me about individual subjects, such as the director of the developmentally disabled theater group, or the teacher who conducts summer school in

her living room. Not by a long shot. The vast majority of people who
came up to me and wanted to talk about television news had one thing
in mind—the exploding whale.

And the truth is, there's not that much story to tell about that old
whale. I'd much prefer to tell them about, say, the two most incredible
golfers I ever met.

———

Stephen Roberts was very serious about his golf but never kept
score. He couldn't—Stephen hadn't learned to count yet. He also
never used a ball washer because he wasn't tall enough to reach one. I'd
heard about him from several people who were mesmerized by
watching this little guy powder the ball with a near-perfect swing.

They'd seen him at golf trade shows and in various golf venues, and
each time this small boy teed it up and hit a few, a crowd would invariably gather to watch.

His mom and dad, Sandy and Dan, told me he'd been in love with
the game his entire life, that he'd watched golf tournaments on television, from start to finish, since he was a baby. That wasn't long before
we met. When we did our first story on Stephen, he was four years old.
He was also very, very small—his weight at the time hadn't yet made
the growth charts, and he was about the size of a two-year old. But his
personality and love of the game were huge.

Like his mother, who uses a wheelchair, Stephen has a condition
called *osteogenesis imperfecta*, or as it's more commonly called, brittle bone
disease. His bones are so fragile that they can break with so much as a
sneeze, and they have. You wouldn't know any of this by looking at
him; his angelic face carries an undefeatable gaze and a perpetual
smile, his big blue eyes magnified by his wire-rimmed glasses, his
blonde hair falling straight around his head. This kid is adorable and
indefatigable, and if you know about the odds he's battling, it's a
delight to watch him run around and play like any happy preschooler.
When I first saw him at the Children's Course in Portland, he was all

business, taking a lesson from instructor Carol Irwin. My cameraman and I found him at the putting green, practicing his chipping, but in the parlance of children's golf instruction, he was actually "hitting the wolf across the river to one of the three pig's houses." Stuffed animals were set about, and Stephen's mission was to get the ball "up" and across "the river," a strip of blue flannel which had been set on the fringe of the green. He was pretty good at it, and barely looked up as we began shooting video, his little club head skimming the grass repeatedly to catch some fairly decent shots.

"Ever since he could stand," his dad told me, "he's picked up a stick or a putter or something, and knocked balls around the floor. That's what he loves to do."

Before we played a few holes together for the camera, his instructor, Carol, asked Stephen what was the most important thing to remember before hitting the ball.

"Have a good setup," he answered without hesitation, a concept lost on many longtime players.

At first, it was hard to watch him swing. I'd never been around anyone with brittle bone disease, but if a sneeze could break a bone, what might a full swing do—perhaps break a lot of things? Still, he seemed to let it rip every time, holding nothing back.

"Stephen's had seven broken femurs," his mother explained to me, "but you can't worry about everything." Sandy also said that doctors believe Stephen's love of golf is what keeps him walking; that people in his condition, like Sandy, generally end up needing the full-time use of a wheelchair. Stephen has need of one occasionally, when his condition worsens or he breaks something major, but rarely when he's around the golf course. There, his spirits soar and his little body seems able to do what it wants.

His play was extraordinary. His tee shots went fifty to seventy-five yards, with that slight right to left turn, or draw, that pros put on the ball. He hit solid irons, his chips and putts displayed a rhythm some golfers work a lifetime to find without success. His mindset—does a kid this young have such a thing?—was all positive, good shot or bad, and his earnest facial expression remained unchanged as he chased after his ball to hit it again.

"He's got it down," said his instructor, Carol. "He's just fantastic. I've never had a student like him."

Our first story on Stephen was so well received—I mean, you can't watch him play and not immediately love him—that we did a follow up story only weeks later. Stephen, unfortunately, had since had a mishap, falling from a park bench and breaking his femur again, this time all of the way through. The injury laid him up, but only for three days, and he was back playing golf again, with the help of a wheelchair and walker.

"He's lost some distance," Carol Irwin explained while watching him play, "but not his naturally good swing. I'd say he's hitting it pretty well."

As they had done before, Stephen's doctors had constructed his leg cast in such a way so that he could keep playing. He would hit the ball from a sitting position in his wheelchair at times, and growing impatient with that, on some shots, stand up, lean into his walker, and swing his little club around it to make contact.

I tried to interview him as we played, but Stephen couldn't much be bothered. Kids notoriously clam up around cameras and microphones, or maybe I don't know the right questions to ask, but I discovered there was another reason for his reticence. Unlike most of us who play golf, he was able to concentrate totally on the game, his next shot taking every bit of his attention. And afterward, his conversation was not about the holes he'd just played, but given exclusively to finding out from his mom and dad precisely when he could play again.

Upon urging, Stephen did tell me that his favorite player was Tiger Woods, and he enthusiastically demonstrated the pro's familiar, victorious arm pump. Unlike Stephen, I thought, Tiger doesn't have to worry about breaking an arm doing it.

"Golf is everything to Stephen," Sandy told us. "It's what keeps him walking, it what keeps him going." Clearly, I've never seen anyone get more out of the game, or play it with greater passion.

Even though I later heard that Stephen had traveled to the Midwest to play in fund-raising tournaments to support people with his condition—finishing quite high in the field I might add—he will never have the physical stature to be a professional player or even a top-ranking amateur. But there will never be a golfer, at any level in the world, who will beat this one small child in attitude. Every pro will tell you that that's the most important part of the game, and Stephen Roberts somehow had it down by the time he was four years old.

————

Jim Taylor is the kind of golfer who could make you mad, if for no other reason than at the time we met to do his story he had eight career holes-in-one. That's quite a number for any player, but unbelievable for a golfer who has no arms or hands.

When he was ten years old, growing up on a farm in Missouri, Jim had a near-fatal encounter with some power lines that were sagging over the roof of the family barn. After he survived the nearly fatal jolt, he was fitted with prostheses and went on with life as if it had never happened.

"In my mind, I got all the parts you have," he explained, "just a few are missing."

Jim's had a number of jobs—at one point, he ran a chain saw in the woods—ending up selling insurance in Washington state. Working on six-month contracts, he had to perform well to keep his job, and by the time he was in his late thirties he had been successful enough to retire. Along the way, he'd also had forty major surgeries.

"In the insurance business, I'd visit all of these resorts and golf courses," Jim said, "and I used to think, I'm going to play that game someday. It just seemed like the ultimate of sports."

He took up golf at thirty-one as a form of therapy, and claims he had an advantage over "normies"—people with all of their original parts—who try to take up the game.

"You can't just try to play golf, it is way too hard," he explained. "You have to make a commitment, and I already had a mindset. I knew I could learn to do this. Most people don't."

We played a hardscrabble par-3 course in an industrial area of Longview, his hometown. Jim is completely unpretentious, and showed up for our round, and his TV story, wearing a cheezy red baseball cap, jeans, and a white T-shirt under a gray, zippered sweatshirt. He was of medium size, on the thin side, had a wispy mustache, and an intense but likeable personality.

He was also the object of plenty of joking by regulars hanging around the course who obviously knew and liked him.

"We keep telling him he'd do better if he'd get his wrists into it," joked one old boy.

"I could beat him hands-down," chimed in another. Jim nodded, smiling, as he headed for the first tee, obviously having heard it all before.

And his game was his real answer. For starters, he used his feet to tee up his ball, something I challenge any golfer to attempt. I've tried it many times since and still can't even get the tee into the ground.

His swing worked perfectly, even though it broke all of the commonly accepted rules. His right-side prosthesis didn't bend when he took the club back, something which has to happen in a normal swing; and coming back down to hit the ball, he transferred the club in midswing from his right hook to a metal device where his left hand would normally be. The device, at the end of his left-side prosthesis, was a piece of metal, like a small half pipe, which he'd crafted to lock into his club's grip. It tore up the grips of his clubs real bad, but allowed him to hang on through impact.

It also allowed Jim to hit some incredibly solid shots, with all of his clubs, or those few he chose to use that day. He didn't like to change clubs much because it was too hard to remove and reattach the gripping device. This resulted in his frequently putting with his pitching wedge, or at times, the back of his wedge, striking the ball from the left side. It was rather maddening to watch him sink several putts, ten to twenty feet in length, using the wrong club, backward. Jim acted as if it was routine.

"The secret to golf," he advised, "is playing your own game. And I feel pretty good about my game. Not too many people are playing it, my way!"

I actually couldn't imagine wanting to play golf without arms or hands, the game is too difficult, but Jim apparently sees golf, and life, differently than most.

"We do have to count our blessings as we go along," he told me. "Basically, remember everything isn't always going to be as bad as you think, no matter how it looks sometimes."

I called Jim Taylor recently after not having a chance to visit with him for a decade or so. Since we'd last talked, he'd had five more surgeries, lowered his golf handicap to eight—which is exactly half the average handicap in America—and raised his hole-in-one total to sixteen. It's enough to make a normie mad.

———

I've played a lot of golf with a lot of people who have a lot of excuses why they don't play better, and I personally maintain several of my own. A Stephen Roberts or a Jim Taylor plays for the love of it, without giving a thought to making excuses or complaining in any way. It's true that no one ever said life, or golf for that matter, is supposed to be fair. But why didn't someone tell us what these two inherently know—that sometimes the pure joy of playing, or of living, is more than enough to get you through.

CHAPTER FIFTEEN

Sam Donaldson and Someone Named Murphy

***

"One of the elders said: 'Either fly as far as you can from men, or else, laughing at the world and the men who are in it, make yourself a fool in many things.'
—*Thomas Merton*

ONE OF THE MISCONCEPTIONS about working in my business is that if you're on television, you're very highly paid.

The most often asked question when I visit local schools to talk about television careers is not about the whale (thankfully), but rather: "How much money do you make?"

Being an American male, of course, I never tell them. The two things every son learns from his father is never to reveal your salary to anyone for any reason, and never to let anyone peek at the bills in your wallet, though I'm not sure why. But back to the point.

Television is like any other industry in that if you work at the highest levels, a top-ten market station or one of the networks, the compensation is very, very good. Veteran news anchors who have been on the air for many years at the same station in major markets also do very well. The rest don't.

On my career-education visits, the figure that I share with inquiring students is whatever the starting salary for a reporter in Portland happens to be. However, most reporters must work for years in much smaller towns before advancing to a market even of Portland's size, and might have to toil for years in Medford or Biloxi for nothing more than the minimum wage.

I can't recall how much I was making in 1970 (and Dad wouldn't want me to tell you if I could), but it wasn't very much. Vicki and I used to be thrilled when a local organization would ask me to give an after-dinner speech because it meant a a free dinner. Likewise, in later years, if a group on the Oregon Coast or elsewhere would ask us to ride in a parade or talk to the annual Chamber of Commerce Banquet, we'd jump at the chance for a weekend getaway, all expenses paid, of course.

One of the ways I earned extra income was to sell the same stories I produced for Channel 2 to our parent network, the American Broadcasting Company. These pieces were never used on ABC's nightly news, but put on something commonly called the DEF, for Daily Electronic Feed, which fed stories each day to all of the affiliate stations for use on their local newscasts.

Since the feed stories needed to be of interest to viewers in other cities, they were often weather related. It might be video of an extreme snowstorm or, in the case of one story I sold, a freak tornado which touched down in Vancouver, Washington. That was of national interest because our part of the country is known for getting major rainfall, not tornadoes. The DEF might also pick up serious spot news stories if the video was good enough, such as a major fire with dramatic scenes of the blaze and rescue attempts. Seasonal stories were also good, like Oregon Christmas trees being loaded into the cargo holds of commercial airliners for transport to buyers in Hawaii.

The DEF editors were also interested in what can only be described as oddities—the farmer's pumpkin that bore an uncanny likeness to Teddy Roosevelt, the man who built a home entirely from beer cans, or the logger who carved remarkable sculptures with a chain saw. (This was before we found out that the woods were full of chain saw sculptors.)

If I could talk the guy on the DEF desk into buying a story, it was an extra $100 each for my photographer and me. You had to learn how to sell your stories; the people at ABC in New York were terse and had little time to hear long explanations of what you were pushing. I worked at developing relationships with the one or two editors who made these decisions, and I never tried to peddle something I didn't honestly feel was worthy.

The whale had to be a slam-dunk. I called ABC first thing Friday morning, even before I'd written our own story for the evening news. The network fed the affiliates their stories at three o'clock in the afternoon, and with the East Coast time difference, I needed to call early to make the DEF line-up. The telephone conversation with the network guy was priceless, another one-of-a-kind experience courtesy of one dead sperm whale.

"Whaddya got?" asked the editor, with a heavy New York accent.

"I got a whale blowing up," I said, which was followed by momentary silence.

"Say that again," said the editor.

I repeated it.

"And what exactly would cause this whale to blow up?" he asked.

"Some State Highway Division workers," I said. Again, brief silence.

"Was this whale in the ocean at the time?" he asked. "And if he was, what were the highway division guys doing in the ocean? Give me the whole thing, here."

I explained the story in full, and—unlike the other conversations I'd had with the ABC folks—I felt I could take my time doing it. The desk man obviously couldn't believe what he was hearing as I parceled it out piece by piece, letting each juicy detail find its mark. I knew I had it sold; this was just for fun.

"And the blubber smacks into this car?" asked the editor, still not buying all of this.

"Flattened it," I said.

"So you're telling me that whale blubber can smash a car."

"It can and it did, and we've got it on film," I said with finality. I could hear him rattle some paper.

"What's your number there?" asked the editor. "I'm needa get back to you."

He hung up abruptly after taking my information. I was stunned to be cut off like that; maybe I'd played it wrong and had been too much of a wise guy in telling the story. Deflated, I forgot about ABC and started to write my story for that evening's newscast. If the network didn't want the most amazing video any affiliate station had ever sent them, that's their problem. What did they know in New York, anyway?

———

Twenty minutes later, as I was ripping a piece of paper out of my Royal typewriter, having failed at coming up with a decent lead (hey, you try writing it!) for the fifth or sixth time, my phone rang.

It was someone else from ABC, not the DEF editor I'd been speaking with.

"You've got an exploding whale story for us?" asked the new network guy.

"Yes, I do," I answered, playing it completely straight this time.

"And I understand you've got on film the actual explosion—what's that look like?"

That was hard to answer without sounding like a smart aleck.

"Well, it looks like your basic explosion," I began, "accept it's mostly red, and you can see chunks of blubber coming down."

"You can actually see it?" he asked.

"Oh yeah, and you can hear it. Hitting the ground and stuff."

Once again, there was momentary silence.

"Listen, we're going to want you to package this for us," he said. "Go ahead and give us a voice track with the network sign-off. Keep the whole piece to 1:20 or so. That work for you?"

"No problem," I said, "but what's my deadline for making the feed?"

"This isn't for the feed," he answered. "We want this for Sam's show on the weekend. Get it to us as fast as you can."

We discussed a few particulars about how I should send the story and to whom, then hung up. I couldn't believe it. As I said, I'd sold a number of stories to ABC for use by their affiliate stations, but I'd never had anything on an actual network newscast.

My story about this completely insignificant, solitary event—the demolition of a deceased mammal on a beach in Oregon—would be seen by millions of Americans on ABC's *Weekend News with Sam Donaldson*.

————

I didn't keep a copy of the network story and, honestly, don't remember how I structured it. I do remember that I didn't appear on camera; we eliminated my stand-up to save time. The piece that I produced for Channel 2's evening news was 3:25 in length, not unusually long back then but way over the top by today's standards, and the network contact had said to keep their story more than two minutes shorter than that. Whatever we sent to New York could have been nothing more than a pared down version of the original.

I narrated a new voice track, Doug edited the new version of the story, and we sent it off, full of anticipation over actually seeing our work on the network.

While I can't recall the story itself, which ran in the Sunday newscast's kicker position, I will never forget the way weekend anchor Sam Donaldson introduced it. If this isn't word for word, it's very close:

"MURPHY'S LAW STATES THAT IF ANYTHING CAN POSSIBLY GO WRONG, IT WILL.

"SOME PEOPLE IN OREGON KNOW JUST WHAT THAT MEANS THIS WEEKEND. THEY TRIED TO BLOW UP A DEAD, BEACHED WHALE WITH DYNAMITE, WITH SOME RATHER SURPRISING RESULTS.

"ABC'S PAUL LINNMAN REPORTS FROM FLORENCE, OREGON."

It was exciting to be introduced as a network correspondent, and Doug and I were happy indeed to watch our work on ABC—the big time, to us. We've talked about the experience many times since, always noting selfishly that it did nothing to actually advance our careers.

But because we'd produced other more important stories, and always questioned the intrinsic value of this one, we've always been a little bemused by the network's putting it before a national audience. The simple reason was that it was an oddity, albeit something anyone could have captured on film, because the story was of no greater value or significance than that. Our conclusion is that it wasn't great video or writing that got us to the network, we just happened to be there when the bomb dropped, as it were.

———

Maybe our reaction is just embarrassment over the fact that we never sold another story of any kind to any ABC news program. When your only shot at getting national exposure as journalists involves putrid blubber flying through the air, and you're not even smart enough to get out of the way, it's kind of insulting, professionally.

Here's the other thing: by now, the exploding whale is arguably the most-watched television news story ever, which brings us to another myth about our business: If something is broadcast repeatedly, like a syndicated situation comedy, the originators of that material become fabulously wealthy, right?

The ABC Television Network paid Doug Brazil $117.50 for his work on the story, and I received $105.00 (Doug had the better union). To date, despite our original story being sold and resold by one outfit or another over the years, that is the sum total of what the two of us have received for having produced it.

———

I've been asked over the years what other news organizations reported on the exploding whale at the time of the incident. Most of the newspapers in the region certainly did, beginning with Florence's *Siuslaw News*.

The two Portland dailies, the *Oregon Journal* and the *Oregonian*, carried their own stories, the latter headlining it: "Blast Fails To Budge Beached Whale, But Sends Blubber Soaring Into Air."

Nearly a full week after the event, the *Oregonian* also reported that the whale was gone, but that the strong odor stayed on. "Some believe the smell lingering on the beach may be the reason seagulls have never arrived to devour the remnant bits of whale as expected," the paper reported.

The *Oregon Journal* story was written by veteran United Press International correspondent Clarence Zaitz. I've been told that the exploding whale was voted Oregon's best wire service story of the year in 1970, and I assume that the Zaitz piece won this honor, because it's the only wire service account I've ever seen.

As for television, I believe it was us alone, and subsequently ABC, who carried the story. Again, people have told me that one of our crosstown rivals in Portland, KGW-TV Channel 8, bought footage of the exploding whale from a freelance photographer on the coast, but I have no recollection of their airing a story on the subject.

I should point out that one other television station, this one in San Francisco, ultimately did broadcast its own version of the exploding whale story, creating quite a stir among viewers in the Bay Area. But they had to borrow our footage to do it, and while their packaging of the story was highly creative, it aired considerably after ours.

Truth be told, it was a quarter century later.

CHAPTER SIXTEEN

Kids, Music, Movies, and Cancer

There are two ways of spreading light: to be the candle,
or the mirror that reflects it.
—*Edith Wharton*

I WAS ANCHORING the news one evening with a young woman who
was my broadcast partner for many years. Her name was Melissa Mills,
and in many ways we fit the mold that many news directors thought
was desirable in the 1980s. Melissa was very bright, attractive, and
young—I'd guess somewhere in her midtwenties; I was about as attractive as a mud fence and in my midforties. We were the perfect
father-daughter team, as seen on TV in many American cities at the
time, a professional news-reading couple, able to leap several
demographic groups in a single bound.

The newscast's lead story concerned a tavern that had been
firebombed in North Portland. One of our talented younger reporters,
Josephine Chang, was on the scene live to report on what had
happened, and our producer directed us to ask Josephine a question
from the set after she wrapped up her report.

What you need to understand about that practice is that nearly all
questions asked by anchorpeople in the studio of reporters live in the
field are scripted, not ad-libbed. This is because all news directors
like their staffs to appear to be all-knowing; heaven forbid that we ask
a question the reporter couldn't answer. I've always disagreed with
that thinking—if a story begged a question that was likely on the

minds of viewers, didn't we look bad by not asking it? And if the reporter didn't have an immediate answer, couldn't she promise to find out and get back to us? That makes us all look good—a vibrant news team, able to anticipate audience thinking and use our resources to respond in their behalf.

I was also a little concerned during this newscast about the question we had been scripted to ask Josephine, "Do authorities know what caused the explosion?" I hadn't had time to question the producer about it in advance, but this information was so basic it seemed Josephine should have covered it early in her report. But never mind, we were on the air, into the story, and I dutifully asked the question about the explosion's cause.

"Well, Paul," Josephine said, looking earnestly into the camera, "there's no official word on what caused it, but there's been specula-tion by police that someone tossed a mazeltov cocktail into the building."

I broke into spontaneous laughter in the studio, my microphone quite open. Unless some celebrating Jewish terrorist who hated taverns was on the loose, I knew the term Josephine had intended to use was "Molotov" cocktail, the homemade incendiary device commonly used by your basic firebomber. Josephine knew that too, I'm sure, but had simply misspoken, as we all do from time to time.

My partner Melissa was all business on the news set, unlike myself, who liked to exchange wisecracks with the camera operators and floor directors during commercial breaks about whatever was happening that day. When I inadvertently laughed at Josephine's mistake on the air, Melissa abruptly dismissed the reporter and led to a commercial, though it wasn't time for a scheduled break.

"What the hell was that about?" she demanded. Melissa, a good reporter who was often criticized for spending too much time on journalistic content and not enough time on her hair—a rare and admirable trait for a broadcast journalist to my thinking—was understandably upset. My reaction had been out of context and unpro-fessional.

"Didn't you hear what Josephine said?" I asked. Melissa shook her head.

"She said mazeltov cocktail," I explained, "when she meant to say Molotov."

"She most certainly did not," Melissa said, in Josephine's defense.

"She did, too," said one of the camera people.

"I don't think she did," said the floor director.

A major group argument ensued and wasn't settled until after the newscast when all present, engineers and technical crew included, marched down to the newsroom to watch a replay of the story. And I was vindicated; sure enough, Josephine had used the wrong word, and she would laugh about it with us later. But no matter how humorous I'd found her malapropism, Melissa was right; my reaction on the air was inappropriate. It wasn't the first or last time I was guilty of such professional misbehavior.

————

The little earpieces that news anchors wear (and which can often be seen by viewers when their cords aren't dressed properly), allow communication between the studio and reporters in the field. They're also used for emergency one-way communication from producers and directors, but the messages must be quick and precise, such as, "Video isn't ready, fill!" or, "Go to break." Any longer communication while the anchor is trying to read the news doesn't work; it's virtually impossible to speak or read words for any length of time while an entirely different set of words is spoken into your ear.

(With the exception of this point, the excellent feature film of some years back, *Broadcast News*, portrayed television news quite accurately, right down to the tape for the lead story being physically run to the tape machine just as the anchor was introducing it on air, a common occurrence. But the movie also had William Hurt's character reading the news, articulating new thoughts, and constructing complex questions for his interview subjects, all while his producer talked to him incessantly through his earpiece. It's just not possible.)

I've heard many humorous stories of the miscommunication that has taken place during newscasts because someone didn't understand what was being said in his or her earpiece, commonly referred to as an "IFB," for "internal feedback device."

My favorite of these concerns an anchor working at a small station in the Midwest who, during a newscast, decided on his own to ask an unscripted question of a reporter live in the field. The reporter didn't hear the question.

"Can you please repeat that, Ralph?" she responded, "my IUD fell out."

Ralph apparently handled the gaffe more professionally than I would have, dutifully repeating his question without so much as cracking a smile. I'm sure I would have lost it.

———————

To me, there is nothing particularly enjoyable or satisfying about sitting in the studio and anchoring the news. I know there are many in our business who consider this the most important part of their work, their very reason for being in the business. I've never felt that way.

While there is a certain excitement to anchoring breaking news for extended periods of time—say, continuing major storm coverage, or an ongoing crime situation such as a gunman in a standoff with police— these are relatively rare. They require you to think on your feet and have basic knowledge of such disparate things as local landmarks, geography, and police procedure. Further, the competent anchor must have a feel for carrying a story and keeping track of all of its parts.

But the simple act of sitting at a desk before a live camera and reading a series of stories someone else has written has no particular appeal for me. There are those in all walks of life who have an inherent desire to be the deliverer of news, to read out loud an interesting item in the newspaper, or to report to friends or family "the latest" on whatever the current hot topic of conversation might be. I guess, theoretically, these people should be doing my job, and I should be home watching them.

Having said that, I have experienced the considerable joy and professional satisfaction that comes from presenting the stories of the scores of inspirational people I have met. Most came to me through the previously mentioned *Spirit of the Northwest* series. It's rewarding to tell the story of an incredible person to an audience of thousands, knowing that there is the possibility that it could lead to life-changing revelations for a few watching. I know it's not the most important work in the world, but it can make a newscaster feel like he's actually contributing to society in a small way.

Many of these story subjects have been youngsters, and among my favorites are two young guys who created ways of communicating their own messages despite the major challenges life had dealt them.

———

Our story on Andy Hordichok—a tall, good-looking college freshman, whose shock of dark hair made him look somehow senatorial—began in a college music rehearsal hall. Andy played saxophone in several different groups but when we visited him he was rehearsing with the Chamber Wind Ensemble of Willamette University in Salem, where he was a student.

Before reaching college, Andy had been awarded just about every honor a young musician could garner. He had won all-state honors, playing in groups that ranged from jazz to the youth symphony, and he had toured internationally as a soloist with honor bands. In short, he was recognized as one of the best high school musicians in the West.

What made Andy Hordichok a unique story subject, however, was that he had achieved all of this despite being almost totally deaf. He was born with a 90 percent hearing loss. The hearing aids that he wore were the only possible tip-offs.

Our story let the ensemble music come up full, then cut to Andy in his home in Portland, playing "Amazing Grace" on his saxophone. His talent was quite obvious, the notes clear and precise, Andy in deep concentration and clearly enjoying making such sweet sounds. But, I wondered, how well could he actually hear them?

"Well," he explained during our interview, "I sense them. I sense the vibrations with my inner self. It's almost like a sixth sense." Andy articulated his words carefully.

I knew that the hearing-impaired often have difficulty speaking, having never clearly heard words spoken themselves, but he had obviously worked at this also. Andy spoke as if he might have had a slight speech impediment, but was easy to understand and very comfortable in conversation.

While my photographer recorded his playing, I talked with his mother about Andy's early years. She said that despite his deafness, he had an immediate affinity for music, first beating on a tambourine as a toddler, then, at the age of six, learning to play the banjo. For our taping, he brought out his banjo and gave us his rendition of that old banjo favorite, the *William Tell Overture!*

We'd also asked one of Andy's music teachers, Joe Wimmer, to drop by during our shoot; I needed someone who knew music to explain how Andy was able to do what he did.

Mr. Wimmer had taught saxophone and clarinet for years in the Portland area, but admitted that when he took Andy on as a student he feared it would be virtually impossible to teach him to play on key. Andy immediately proved him wrong.

"What I learned from him," the teacher explained, "is how much we unconsciously sense what we're doing when we play an instrument. And we just take this for granted."

And that's pretty much how Andy explained it.

"I have to sense it," he said, "there's no other way I can explain it. It's just the most difficult thing to explain to others."

I guess Andy explained it best with his playing, and he also shared his music philosophy and knowledge with young students he taught in the basement of his family's home. We watched and listened to Andy play a duet with a middle school youngster, the two of them sitting before a wall that was virtually covered with the plaques and awards Andy had won with his music. What had to make him an effective teacher was his unflagging belief that if he could learn to play an instrument, anyone could.

"One can do anything no matter what the challenge," he told us, "as long as they put their mind to it and do it."

No question, Andy Hordichok proved it to be true—a deaf person who said he couldn't imagine a world without music. He is unique among the thousands of feature subjects I've covered, in that I never fully comprehended how he was able to do what he did. I didn't have to—all I had to do was listen.

———

There was nothing wrong with Chris Buckmaster's hearing. His problem was cancer, and life had thrown him a double dose of it.

When we met, Chris was a senior at Reynolds High School in the town of Troutdale, east of Portland. He was a big, burly kid, his head completely bald, his facial features puffed up unnaturally by the effects of his cancer treatments. He was friendly and soft-spoken, seemingly not bitter at all about beating cancer as a very young child, only to have it come back in his teen years in the form of a brain tumor.

Chris explained to us that he had always wanted to be a filmmaker. He'd actually gotten to work on a couple of films shot in Portland, as a grip and lighting assistant. His bedroom was filled with movie memorabilia, including a miniature, highly detailed set he had constructed for an animated short film.

But now he had a new goal in mind. Since he'd already been through it once and was now going through it again, Chris Buckmaster had decided to make a movie to show other families how to get through the devastating experience of cancer.

"I think I can help them," he told me on camera. "I want to show how it's all about family support and positive attitudes. That's the message."

Chris was nineteen, and it was difficult to understand how he would reach his goal. I had met many aspiring filmmakers who had never achieved their dream of making a movie because there were too many obstacles. Chris was very sick and undergoing regular treatments for his own cancer. But he was already well on his way with his film project.

He had somehow persuaded two professional Portland filmmakers, Corky Miller and Paul Ramsey, to help him make his movie.

We went with them to the studios of Oregon Public Broadcasting in Portland, where Chris would do his first interviews with the experts he had assembled to appear in his film. Our camera followed him as he moved about the studio, adjusting the lighting, conferring with Corky and Paul, and looking through the viewfinder of his camera to check shots. He appeared to know what he was doing, and there was no question about what he wanted his picture to convey.

"Everything," he said. "I want to tell families how to deal with everything when someone gets cancer, and especially, how they can still enjoy life every day."

The more we watched Chris work, and heard what he had to say, the more we realized he was going to pull it off, even as he fought cancer himself. His mother told us she thought it was his love of film and wanting to reach that goal that helped him keep going in life. Further, she said she believed it was Chris's attitude that had kept the entire family going through this second time around with cancer.

"He's a fighter," said Chris's dad, on camera. "He doesn't give in, no matter what. He just keeps pushing toward his goals."

As evidence of this, we learned during the shooting of our story that Chris had somehow persuaded actor Paul Newman to help finance his movie.

We revisited Chris for a second story a few months later, his documentary film, titled *The 'C' Word*, having been completed. With consultation from his two filmmaking friends, Chris wrote, produced, and directed the entire picture, and it's a remarkable piece of work.

The film begins with Chris sitting somewhere in the Oregon countryside. The camera circles him as he watches a sunset. We hear his words: "When I found out I had cancer, it really shocked me a lot." It's a compelling start—you want to hear this kid's story.

The documentary visits other cancer patients, doctors, counselors, and parents, and results in a remarkably honest look at a deadly disease from the perspective of those who live with it, personally or professionally, every day.

A teenage girl, a cancer patient, looks directly into the camera and says: "You're not the only one. There are millions of us out there. And make sure you stay close with your family. They're your number one thing, your number one support group."

We see Chris undergoing a cancer treatment (for all of the times you've heard of chemotherapy, have you ever seen anyone actually experience what it is?), and hear him say: "Sometimes cancer treatment can make you feel even sicker. It helps a lot to know what to expect."

There is one scene in the film that's impossible to forget, and for me it means tears each time I see it.

Chris and his dad, Steve, are sharing a quiet moment in a treatment room waiting for Chris's next round of chemotherapy. The dialogue is very soft, and the listener must concentrate to hear their brief exchange.

"As long as you're here and walking around, then I got you," says his dad. "That's what counts to me."

Chris purses his lips, as if trying to be strong, not wanting to cry, but he's close.

Father and son lean into one another, clasping each other's hands.

"Yeah," Chris says, an acknowledgment of what they both know. Chris is going through some terrible stuff, but he's still alive. And he's not alone.

"I love you, Dad," says Chris.

"I love you, too," responds Steve. "Be tough, kid. Keep up the good work."

There rest of the scene is silent, there's no more talking, as the camera holds on the two of them for several seconds. Father and son are simply looking directly at one another, their hands still stacked together. Nothing more needs to be said. It is a powerful moment, and for all of the stories of cancer patients viewers may have heard from their friends and loved ones, they've never experienced anything like this.

When I asked Chris, in our story, why he had felt so compelled to make his movie, he said he just felt he had to let other families know not only how to deal with cancer, but also how to enjoy life while doing it.

His film ends as it began, with Chris watching the sunset. The camera moves around him, catching him in profile, the sun playing nice tricks with light and shadow. And again, we hear Chris's voice.

"And you've got to make the best of every day. You only have one life to live, make every day good."

Chris's film is now given to all of the cancer patients and families who come to Doernbecher Children's Hospital in Portland for treatment. Administrators say that it is invaluable in presenting vital information in a way that they cannot.

I don't know of a moviemaker who has made a more important film.

CHAPTER SEVENTEEN

Three Guys Who Kept the Whale Alive

When there are two conflicting versions of a story, the wise course is to believe the one in which people appear at their worst.
—*H. Allen Smith,* Let the Crabgrass Grow, *1960*

THE REQUESTS FROM VIEWERS and others for copies of our original exploding whale story were, at best, sporadic for the first several years.

Television newsrooms are continuously contacted by persons who feel a great need, for one reason or another, to obtain copies of stories that aired either the night before or sometime in the past. To be frank, most callers are given short shrift; there's no one around, editor or reporter, who has the time or the inclination to chase down the video in question, make a dub, and mail it off. Further, no one feels an obligation to do so, since the single daily priority is producing that night's newscast. Some stations strictly enforce policies against sharing news video for any purpose; others may refer callers to licensed video dubbing services in cities where they exist.

(You can be sure that if there was substantial money to be made from doing it, every television station in America would have its own "News Video R Us" department, and send out cassettes by the truckload. It must not pencil out.)

Whatever calls Doug and I first received about the whale went largely ignored. We would mention such requests to one another, have a laugh over why anyone could possibly want their own copy of the story, and forget about it. In fact, when the time came that the demand for whale dubs grew beyond the point of being ridiculous, and our own television station wanted the story for its Web site, we couldn't even find a copy. Fortunately, Doug learned of a station in Texas that had one, and we were able to get what had to be a third- or fourth-generation dub of our own story.

But long before this, and unbeknownst to us, things were happening that indeed worked to keep the exploding whale story from dying. Three men, working in vastly different fields in various parts of the country, unknowingly conspired to create worldwide interest in what had happened in Florence, Oregon, on November 12, 1970. One was a news media headhunter, another a nationally syndicated columnist, the third a public affairs coordinator with the Oregon Department of Transportation.

Nearly everyone in broadcasting pays attention to an insider information source called *ShopTalk*. It began as a subscriber electronic bulletin board, but continues today on the Internet as the longest-running newsletter devoted exclusively to the broadcast industry. Its founder is a guy named Don Fitzpatrick, a talent scout who's been following and writing about industry trends since the early 1970s.

The letters section of the *ShopTalk* issue of October 27, 1994, carried the following message from one Kevin Crane, who identified himself as an executive producer at WGBY-TV in Springfield, Massachusetts:

"Don, This came to me through a friend who got it from a friend who got it from a friend.... I don't know who to attribute it to, but everyone at the station loved the story. I thought *ShopTalk* readers would like it too."

As the undertaker said when he first tried to place the left leg of the man who wrote "The Hokey Pokey" into a casket, that's when the trouble started!

Crane had forwarded, and Fitzpatrick printed, a humorous story about Oregon's exploding whale. While most of it was accurate, the information was embellished and exaggerated just enough to create a very funny account of what had taken place on that November day in 1970.

Here's how its writer, who was not identified in any way, described the moment of the actual explosion:

> *So they moved the spectators back up the beach, put a half-ton of dynamite next to the whale, and set it off. I am probably guilty of understatement when I say that what follows, on the videotape, is the most wonderful event in the history of the universe. First you see the whale carcass disappear in a huge blast of smoke and flame. Then you hear the happy spectators shouting "Yayy!" and "Whee!" Then, suddenly, the crowd's tone changes. You hear a new sound, more like "splud." You hear a woman's voice shouting "Here come pieces of . . . my God!" Something smears the camera lens.*

Of course, nothing smeared our camera lens, though it surely was coated with blubber mist, and the sound was more of a "thunk" than a "splud" when pieces started hitting the ground, but all and all, the account was good and very funny.

It was followed by parenthetical comments from the editor, presumably Fitzpatrick: "Kevin, we would love to see a copy of the reporter's tape. We also wonder if the person who dreamed up this scheme for the Oregon Highway Division also worked at WKRP in Cincinnati, during their 'Thanksgiving Live Turkey Shopping Center Giveaway?' You may recall Herb threw live turkeys from a helicopter into a crowd of waiting listeners."

That might have been the end of it, but the very next day, Fitzpatrick had gained more information and reported as a follow-up that the whale story "appears to be true." After confirming a few facts of the event, without identifying his source, Fitzpatrick does inform his readers that the previous day's "Tale of the Whale" account was penned by *Miami Herald* writer and nationally syndicated humorist Dave Barry. It was further noted that the piece first appeared in one of his columns (in May of 1990) and later in a book compilation.

"The item was then posted on the Internet," the *ShopTalk* item explains, "and it's been floating around for about three years there." Fitzpatrick further reported that a CNN producer had unsuccessfully tried to track down a videotape copy of the story, surmising correctly that it may have been originally recorded on film and speculating it may have not been saved on videotape.

Fitzpatrick concludes with an appeal to his readers: ". . . if this whale story does exist visually somewhere—we would love to have it. You know where to reach us."

———

Three days later, what was becoming a media detective story appeared close to being solved. (I could have made this a whole lot easier for Don Fitzpatrick and his friends, but am not a regular *ShopTalk* reader, and I wasn't aware at the time of the whale story's serialization in the newsletter.)

The October 31, 1994, newsletter stated: "Whale of a Story Update: THE TAPE EXISTS!!! We've talked to at least four people who have seen the tape and two of them have copies, which are winging their way to us—even as you read this. The whale event was filmed in the early 1970s and then eventually transferred to video. We'll give you a blow (hole) by blow (hole) description later this week."

After this, *ShopTalk* heard from other correspondents who had seen the video, including a few who had accurately attributed it to Doug and me and our television station in Portland. On November 7, 1994, a writer for the first time identified where the exploding whale story could be downloaded from the Internet (ftp cathouse.org), and the worldwide rush to obtain this bizarre piece of video was apparently on. Remarkably, our little story could ultimately be found in one form or another on more than a thousand Web sites, but this was the start of it all.

There was another person who at the outset could have given Don Fitzpatrick and his readers everything they wanted to know about the exploding whale incident. Ed Schoaps, at the time a community relations coordinator in the Oregon Transportation Division's public affairs office, not only knew the entire story, he wrote his own version of it.

"Sometime around the spring of 1994," Ed explained, "I started getting phone calls and e-mails from different people around the country, asking, 'Is it true you guys blew up this whale?'" He did a little research, obtained a dub of our story, and located the humorous account that was being circulated on the Internet.

"I figured it had to be Dave Barry," Schoaps said, "because it was definitely his style and began with Barry's signature line, 'I'm not making this up.'" At the time he discovered the article, Schoaps, a bright guy who is the antithesis of the nerdy bureaucrat and who still works in public affairs at ODOT, was looking for something fun to write for the monthly employee newsletter. He had found his subject.

"One thing I know is that most people don't view government employees as having much of a sense of humor," he explained. "I just thought this would make a really great article for our employees and others to read, one that kind of puts a human face on ODOT and the highway department."

Schoaps's bosses, at least initially, disagreed. "When I first gave it to them for review before it was published," Schoaps said, "they all looked at me like I was from Mars." But after making his argument, and also pointing out that the transportation division itself was by that time using the whale explosion video as an icebreaker at employee training sessions, his story was good to go.

It appeared in the ODOT newsletter, *TranScript*, in July of 1994, under the headline, "The great blubber storm of 1970 lives on." To this day, Schoaps good-naturedly questions the editors' placement of his piece on page two, noting that page one was given to an article on an executive order concerning state business. "I mean, how boring is that?" Schoaps rightfully asks.

His story is very well written, pointing out that "the flying blubber incident survives as an Oregon legend, kept alive by a film-video of the event that has found its way as far as a Washington, D.C., think tank." Schoaps, who has spent his entire career working with writers and reporters from all media, is unequivocal in stating his view that the incident created "one of the most interesting stories ever reported in newspapers, on radio and TV."

More importantly, his article clarified what served to keep the story alive then and continues to keep it alive today: wherever it is reported, the "when" of the story is invariably omitted. The electronic bulletin board articles that inspired the Schoaps newsletter story; the *ShopTalk* piece; the columnist for the *Daily News* in Moscow-Pullman, Idaho/Washington who reprinted one of the Internet stories word for word; the *World's Most Amazing Videos* program on NBC, which broadcast the exploding whale nationally as recently as 1999; none of these and few others make clear that the incident took place more than a quarter century ago. Thus, those hearing about it for the first time pass the story on as if it had happened yesterday, and the whale is given new life.

Ed Schoaps sent a copy of his article to Don Fitzpatrick, who reprinted it in full in his newsletter. It is worthy of note that the Schoaps article, which has been titled "Son of Blubber" in the various places it's been reprinted over the years, concluded with this telling epilogue: "When a pod of forty-one sperm whales washed ashore in nearly the same location in 1979, State Parks officials burned and buried them."

What kind of response did Ed's article receive after it appeared in the transportation department's official newsletter?

"ODOT employees started calling me for copies of the videotape immediately," he laughed. "So I started getting more requests for dubs."

He also believes publishing the story accomplished his goal of "humanizing" his fellow state workers.

"If you can't look at your own organization with a sense of humor," Schoaps explains, "something's wrong." Pointing out that his department has used the whale video for a variety of training purposes in addition to its use as a conference "icebreaker," Schoaps believes it confirms a useful understanding for ODOT employees.

"What do you do when you find yourself in a situation you would rather not be in?" he asks. "All you can do is shake your head and laugh and say, 'Well, it happened!'"

———

Since Doug Brazil and I were not remotely interested in keeping alive the whale story beyond its initial telling on our newscast of 1970, it could be argued that Don Fitzpatrick, Dave Barry, and Ed Schoaps have been responsible for what can only be described as the worldwide curiosity in this singular event. And I'm quite sure it won't subside anytime soon. This is because Dave Barry, the best known and most widely read player in this distinguished group of blubber aficionados, is not finished with the subject. Not by a long shot.

CHAPTER EIGHTEEN

Toilet-Paper Philanthropy

"You know very well that love is,
above all, the gift of oneself!"
—*Jean Anouilh*, Ardele, *1949*

HERE IS THE NUMBER ONE THING people in Portland say to me repeatedly in public, because they've seen me on television since they were old enough to watch television:

"Hey, I see you on TV!"

Here's the second-most common thing people in Portland say to me for the same reason:

"Hey, you're Paul Linnman."

In all of the years that I've been so greeted, I haven't developed a good answer to either. It doesn't help that they're always presented as new information, as if I didn't know that I was 1) on television, and 2) Paul Linnman. Since I don't wish to disappoint anyone who thinks they are helping me out by imparting such knowledge, my standard reply to each has come to be a wimpy "Yeah," usually followed by a self-conscious laugh. My greeters then immediately look as if they were sorry they said anything at all, and we part ways feeling rather uncomfortable for having had the exchange.

Viewer comments have also changed as I've aged on television.

Here's the number one thing attractive young women used to say to me in public:

"Hey, my mother watches you all of the time."

Here's the number one thing attractive young women now say to me in public:

"Hey, my grandmother watches you all of the time."

Anyone who works in the public eye and claims that they don't enjoy being recognized is a liar. It is nice to have strangers in the supermarket realize who you are and say hello—and, in Portland anyway, people are very nice about respecting your privacy. They tend not to approach your table in a restaurant when you're dining with your family, and when walking down the street I'm aware of many more people who recognize me from the news and don't say anything at all than those who do.

I will say, however, that after thirty-five years of doing television in one market, it can wear on you at times. If you're in Albertson's early on a Sunday morning to buy milk for your oatmeal before you've even had a cup of coffee or showered, you'd prefer that the nice young lady not walk up and report how much her grandmother likes watching you on television. And it can be a lot harder on your loved ones than it is on you. How many times have my wife and children had to stand in the mall and listen to a viewer tell me how wonderful I am, knowing full well that only a half hour before I had overreacted to some stupid thing and been a complete jerk to them?

And I fully realize that I'm just a little guppy in a little puddle. I can't imagine what nationally known news and talk show types, like Peter Jennings or Barbara Walters or Oprah Winfrey, must experience as they move about in public, though I suspect there are parts of the recognition thing that they enjoy as well. Conversely, I can't imagine what life must be like for an internationally known superstar, a Tiger Woods or Britney Spears. All of that wealth and fame can't be worth giving up the freedom of living a normal life, can it? Only they know for sure.

One thing I know for certain: there's an uninvited greeting that I hear frequently from strangers that no one else in the world ever experiences. People delight in mentioning to me our friend the dearly dynamited whale.

A recent exchange took place at the golf course. Over the years, I've taken to playing dawn golf; a group of us who coached our kids couldn't give up an entire Saturday for our weekly golf game, so we took to getting the earliest tee-times available. (In late June we actually start as early as 4:52 AM, and by 8:30 or so, we've played eighteen holes and are on our way home, the entire day still ahead!)

Not long ago I was walking into the clubhouse of one of our favorite municipal courses well before sunup, and encountered another golfer who cheerfully said: "Good morning, Paul. Allow me to be the first today to ask if you've blown up any whales lately!"

I just as happily informed him that he was the third. Well, maybe they didn't ask the question in that precise manner, but two guys in Starbucks had asked me about the whale only minutes before when I'd stopped for coffee. "You've got to get up pretty early," I advised the golfer, who had suddenly turned glum. Maybe I should have just let him have his fun.

And I can only recall one situation in which people mentioned the whale to me in a less than friendly way. In January of 1996 I covered the arrival of Keiko the killer whale, star of the *Free Willy* movies, at the Oregon Coast Aquarium in Newport, Oregon. A few spectators were sincerely shocked to see me.

"What are you doing here?" snapped an elderly lady in a plastic rain bonnet. "You're not going to try to blow up this whale, too, are you?" She didn't say it in a joking way, and even I felt at least momentarily like I had come to the party without an invitation, or had a stick of dynamite sticking out of my pocket.

Having by now produced thousands of stories on wonderful people who have done significant things in their lives, I can't say how many times I've wished that a viewer would come up to me and mention one of them, rather than the whale. Why couldn't just one person say something like, "Hey, aren't you Paul Linnman, the guy who put The Toilet Paper Lady on television?"

I have never known anyone who has done more with less to help so many than Donna Lynn Kublick.

We met in the summer of 1994, about three years after Donna Lynn was put on swing shift at the national transportation company where she worked as a supervisor. It was then that she noticed that the night-time janitors were removing partially used rolls of toilet tissue from the company's rest room stalls.

"I finally asked a janitor, 'what do you do with those?'" Donna Lynn related in a story interview, "and she said they put them in the trash."

Donna Lynn decided to ask her supervisors if, on her own time, she could take the quarter rolls of tissue to local helping organizations. She was given permission to do so.

It wasn't long before she could be seen traveling Portland's freeways in her compact car, the inside filled to the ceiling and all around its driver with clear plastic bags filled with partially used rolls of toilet tissue. People would laugh and wave, which Donna said made her feel even better about what she was doing, as she made her regular deliveries, first to a shelter for battered women, then to a youth center used by street kids. It wasn't long before everyone at work, and some at the agencies, started calling Donna Lynn "The Toilet Paper Lady."

People at the charities were sincerely grateful. "We depend very heavily on donations from people in the community," one of the organization's directors told me. "Donna Lynn has filled a need that other people don't think of sometimes." She also said the donations, though seemingly small, actually made a financial impact, freeing budgeted funds to pay for other necessities.

Donna Lynn seemed just right for the job, a good-natured sort, an obviously thoughtful person I estimated to be in her thirties, and the type coworkers would want to spend time with. And soon, after learning of her TP deliveries, her fellow employees caught Donna Lynn completely by surprise; they started bringing other donated items—clothing, blankets, even food—to her desk at work.

Donna Lynn enlisted the aid of another volunteer to sort and gather all of the contributions. "And I started telling everyone," she explained, "when you clean that closet, you don't even have to take it out of the car—we'll get it to where it's needed."

Before long, she found herself making four deliveries a week and had trouble keeping ahead of the items piling up in her office. She recruited still more volunteers to help, and loved the feeling that their giving brought.

"It makes me feel wonderful," she told me. "Once they do it, they're like me, they're hooked, hooked. It makes you feel so good in the heart."

Meeting Donna Lynn Kublick reminded me of a story I'd done a couple of years before on a completely different type of giver.

Robert Pamplin Jr. was one of Portland's most successful businessmen, a corporate giant and a millionaire many times over. He was at the top of a number of thriving companies, involved with manufacturing, textiles, sand and gravel, and agricultural products. A likeable gentleman with family roots in the South, Bob Pamplin was also known as one who gave back to the community, a dedicated philanthropist—and a creative one, to boot.

After winning a bout with cancer years before, Bob told me he had decided to redirect his life. A lifelong Christian, he wanted to strengthen his relationship with God and find ways to better serve his fellow man.

Always one to "not just to jump in the pond, but find the deep end and do the whole thing in one full swoop," he went back to school and earned his doctorate in ministry, then founded a church. One of its primary missions was to feed the hungry.

"I really believe that patriotism, integrity, honesty, and doing what is right are just shadows of words when a person is starving," he explained.

The food ministry was based at Pamplin's Columbia Empire Farms, near Sherwood, Oregon, where some of the food for the poor was grown and stored. Using what he called "innovative economics," much of the rest of the food was purchased from other manufacturers at a fraction of retail cost. What's more, Bob Pamplin was proud to point out all of the food items were of the highest quality.

"If we offer food that's of low quality," he said in our story, "we're telling these people that we truly believe that they are of low quality. And once again we reinforce in their minds what they've already been made to believe about themselves."

At the time we met, Bob Pamplin's ministry was delivering about one million pounds of food annually to people of all ages through thirty-eight different agencies throughout the Pacific Northwest. Bob told us he didn't think it was much and that he believed more could be done.

"To see someone being given such a little bit, and it means so much to them, it's just very humbling," he told me.

———————

I couldn't help but measure what I witnessed Bob Pamplin doing in the community against Donna Lynn Kublick's contributions, concluding that there was no real difference between the two. Both had found creative ways to give back to others according to how much they could do and where they were in life. I was aware of the old saying that "Much is asked of those to whom much is given," but was also convinced that one needn't be given much to give back a lot.

Pamplin, one of America's corporate leaders, told me that he gets much in return from his contributions, and that he had learned that using his God-given talent to serve others is the best business of them all. Donna Lynn said much the same thing, relating that her efforts had changed her life, inside and out.

Several months later, we did a second story on Donna Lynn Kublick. After her one-woman distribution center expanded to include the efforts of several volunteer employees, her employer wanted in on the act. The company decided to expand the program and give it their official stamp of approval, naming Donna Lynn full-time community volunteer coordinator.

Donna Lynn told us she was still driving around a car full of TP, but also other things she had never dreamed of. Her company donated surplus office products, and Donna Lynn found herself delivering computers to inner-city schools, doorknobs to Habitat for Humanity, and chairs to any organization that needed them.

Best of all, she was sending people to where they were needed. Her operation grew to the point of providing supplies and volunteers to some fifty agencies in Oregon and Southwest Washington. Her industry honored her with international recognition for her efforts, but Donna Lynn gave the credit to her coworkers and her bosses.

"For this company to open its doors and say, 'Yes, we are going to help more and give you the freedom to develop the program'—it has just been heaven."

There was a second story on Robert Pamplin Jr., too. A local college needed money to expand its cramped library, and Bob had committed to donating $1 million to the cause, but not necessarily as an outright gift.

A serious physical fitness advocate, he challenged students to out-perform him in a series of exercises; for each student who could climb a 16-foot rope in 15 seconds, or do 116 push-ups without stopping, or 625 sit-ups in 15 minutes (to name just a few of the challenges), he would donate $25,000 in their name to the library expansion—up to the $1 million.

College officials anticipated that relatively few students would take Bob up on the challenge, but by the day of the competition a thousand participants had signed up for multiple events—students, faculty, and administrators, all dedicated to "Beat Bob."

"I have never seen anything on this campus that has brought the community together like this has," observed one college official.

Bob Pamplin had to know what was coming when he issued the challenge.

"Years from now," he told us, "I want these people to look back on their accomplishment and say, 'That was one of the highlights of my life; I built that library, that was a part of me.'"

––––––––––

Oftentimes I think about the extreme wealth in our society, and how many who control it don't always choose to share even a little with those in need. I think of the "I've got mine" group, who would rather watch needed schools close than vote the tax increases necessary to keep them open. I watch stories about the latest trends, gadgets, cars, fashions, electronics, you name it, that most of us—myself included—waste our hard-earned money on in the hope that the next item will finally lead to happiness. Such thoughts can be depressing.

But then I remember the Toilet Paper Lady and The Push-Up Philanthropist, and I realize what is possible when people who care about others decide to do something about it. That's a whale of a message.

Chapter Nineteen

Where the Arts and Marine Biology Meet

I not only heard the story, I invented it.
—Mark Twain

REQUESTS FOR COPIES of our exploding whale story began to increase dramatically sometime in the early 1990s. For years we had heard from those curious types who learn about something offbeat in the media and have to pursue it for themselves, but they were relatively few in number, and Doug Brazil dealt with each inquiry as he saw fit. But the inquiries increased to the point that they could no longer be ignored. People also wanted to talk to us personally about the whale. The subject was constantly mentioned to us as we covered other stories, and I was always surprised when the underlying question of many, even those who had *seen* the story, seemed to be "Did that really happen?" Could it have been that we had lost all credibility with our earlier story on the two-headed dog? That wasn't likely—we were only asked about the dog for a couple of weeks before it seemed to be completely forgotten by our viewing public.

The first indication that people far and wide were still very interested in the whale came when Doug was contacted by an organization that hosted an annual event in South Carolina.

"The thing that amazed me about it was that it was some kind of arts festival or conference," Doug remembers. "They sent a brochure and everything but I was really taken aback because I couldn't imagine why anyone would want to see a whale blow up at an arts festival."

Nonetheless, Doug dutifully sent the video to the Spoleto Festival in Charleston, South Carolina, and we logically concluded that festival-goers that year were treated to a little "performance art" in the form of a strange piece of film from Oregon.

Also about this time, Dave Barry, one of America's most widely read humorists, wrote his first column on the whale. His account was pirated on a variety of Web sites, in most cases under the title of "The Farside Comes to Oregon," opening the floodgates. For the next decade and beyond (at least, until such time that the exploding whale footage could be found on virtually hundreds of Web sites), the requests for copies came almost daily. They were fielded by both Doug Brazil at our television station in Portland and, to a lesser degree, by Ed Schoaps at the Department of Transportation in Salem.

At first—like with Doug's reaction to the arts festival people— we were surprised by who wanted to see the story and obtain their own copy. We heard from major universities and schools at all levels, all branches of the military, more bomb disposal and hazmat crews than you could shake a stick of dynamite at, a variety of television programs, marine biology conferences, major corporations, national testing laboratories, the offices of U.S. senators, NASA, the Federal Aviation Administration, and most of the other branches of the federal government.

Requests came from as far away as Great Britain, Germany, Japan, and New Zealand, and, as time passed, Doug and I continued to be surprised by what we'd started. Since we were both receiving inquiries, we would pass the better requests back and forth, fascinated by who was asking and why, and how they'd heard about our insignificant little story.

Specific categories of requests soon emerged, beginning with government or military types who asked for dubs for "training" purposes.

"I believe there is a use for this story in the interest of the U.S. Army," wrote Lt. William Mizell of the Army's Armament Research Center in New Jersey. "Since the nature of our business deals in armaments and explosives, we feel that having the opportunity to view your video footage of the explosion could be used as a learning tool for what 'not to do' in a similar situation."

An emergency planning specialist for the Michigan State Police suggested a slightly different use in making his request. "Although the story does not depict an emergency," wrote Curtis Irish, "it certainly points out the need to properly plan activities ahead of time. The humorous aspects of the story will be a nice departure from traditional examples of planning available for classroom presentation."

Mike Nolan of the Illinois State Police bomb squad advised us that he had actually seen the video at a hazardous materials technicians course at the University of Illinois Fire Institute in Champaign. He obtained his own "poor copy" for use during bomb squad training, which he said was "always received very well," but was in need of a better dub, which he indicated would also be shared with another organization, the Explosive Ordinance Disposal Unit of Scott Air Force Base. "Once they get a copy," Mike wrote, "heaven knows where it might end up."

Some of the letters contained humor, some were straightforward. "We intend to use the video copy in Explosive Training and Total Quality Management Training for the 184 Bomb Wing," wrote MSgt. Brian Kuder of the Kansas Air National Guard, and that sounded pretty important to us.

Equally terse was an inquiry from the NASA–Johnson Space Center in Houston. "The first usage of the tape will be during a safety presentation on October 23, 1996," wrote engineer Todd Hinkel. Both organizations got their dubs—how can you turn down a bomb wing, or NASA? We felt much the same about the letters we received from the Departments of Defense and Transportation.

Like the bomb squad guy from Illinois, many correspondents had already seen the video in other training sessions and now wanted it for their own use.

"I viewed the video during recurrent Aircraft Accident Investigation in Oklahoma City," advised Howard Manning of the Federal Aviation Administration. He wanted to use the footage "to supplement a pilot safety meeting on crew resource management and human error. Also for FAA inspector training on Accident Investigation and rules of evidence and forms of evidence." Okay with us.

Among the most curious of requests in the government/military category was one we received from an engineer assigned the task of converting the Georgia Department of Transportation to the metric system. "You may ask what a 'whale blubber' story has to do with Metrics," put forth Kathryn Stansell, explaining that she hoped "it would provide some humor in our training, and also a parallel as to how we can sometimes 'underestimate' ourselves." We liked that inquiry, and sent the dub right off, as we did with almost all correspondents who went light on the "official" reasons for wanting the footage and stressed its humorous appeal.

Personally, and perhaps because my own educational background is not that sterling, I favored the letters we received from universities and educational conferences, my all-time favorite being one from the Eleventh Biennial Conference on the Biology of Marine Mammals, held in Orlando, Florida.

The letter from conference chair Daniel K. Odell seemed to give our story newfound respectability: "Since the 'explosion' is somewhat of a unique event in the marine mammal world, I would like to obtain a copy of the original broadcast to show at the conference. I expect about fifteen hundred attendees from all over the world. I know that the video would add a unique touch to the conference."

Of course, the gathering, sponsored by (ahem), the Society for Marine Mammalogy, and hosted by both Sea World and the Hubbs–Sea World Research Institute, received its copy posthaste.

And unlike just about every other organization requesting a copy, Dr. Odell sent a thank-you letter following his use of the video.

"We had almost sixteen hundred people in attendance from all over the world," he reported. "This was the largest conference we have ever had. A new generation of marine mammalogists was exposed to your classic coverage of the explosion." Beautiful.

We think that's what also led to a spate of international requests, though not all necessarily from the marine research field.

"Can you stand another inquiry about the famous whale videotape?" wrote Sharon Domier of the Miyazaki Educational Institution Library in Japan. "Our anthropology professor would like to use a copy of the videotape in his class on urban legends vs. fact."

But most of the educators asking for copies were from here in the good old USA, and we were also rather flattered by their inquiries. Susan Radford, a science teacher at North Middle School in Everett, Washington, was representative of many who wrote us. "The reason I am requesting this video," she stated, "is to provide students with an intriguing, real-life situation that correlates with the recent revisions of the Washington State Science standards. I believe this would be a positive way to stimulate critical thinking skills in my students." Doug and I were pleased to learn that our twenty-five-year-old story fit right in with recently revised teaching standards in science.

But our favorite educational request came from a computer science professor at the University of Massachusetts in Amherst. Dr. William Verts wrote that "the classic clip of the 'exploding whale' news report" would be used in a series of lectures he was taping on computer literacy "to be broadcast to various university sites in Africa. I have a section on multimedia," Dr. Verts explained, "where I show computer based audio and video."

Whatever. Doug and I were thrilled with the idea of computer students in Africa viewing this bizarre news story from the Oregon Coast. What kind of conversations, we wondered, might result?

Requests from business and industry were not as numerous as those from government and education, but they were no less interesting.

"I work as a consultant for Shell Oil," wrote Dan Taylor. "We have used the Web page 'QuickTime movie' as a meeting opener to introduce things like pre-job planning and communication. It's always a hit."

We received corporate requests from such diverse concerns as Microsoft and the United States Sugar Corporation, the latter's environmental compliance manager advising that he needed a dub for his "safety training." An exploding whale applicable to safety training at a sugar company? It seemed quite a stretch, but Doug said he liked the guy's name—Chester H. Wendell, III—and his request was granted.

Various departments at the Boeing company felt compelled to ask for copies, but the most creative request came from a guy who ran a program for the aircraft maker called Plane Talk About Leadership. In his letter, Phil Polizatto explained that this was "an FAA mandated course for all pilots, which emphasizes how the captain's behavior affects the rest of the crew and thus the safety of the flight."

Thinking about all of those pilots watching the whale blow up as an exercise in advancing their own behavior was captivating, but Mr. Polizatto's further comments made it even more compelling.

"One of the primary components of Plane Talk," he wrote, "is the Problem Solving/Decision Making module. In it we discuss traps to decision making, one of which is called 'representativeness.' I have come across no finer example of this trap than the film you made about the whale on the Florence, Oregon, beach." Doug and I had no idea what "representativeness" might have been or how the whale might be an example of it, but we liked the letter and sent a copy to Seattle.

Time after time we were also able to track how sending a dub to one outfit led to requests from several others. Janet Sadler, for instance, an executive with an aviation insurance concern in London, heard about the whale from colleagues at Boeing. We absolutely loved her explanation of why she wanted the whale.

"I am addressing an aviation/space insurance conference in Copenhagen, Denmark, at the end of this month and think that the video

would make an excellent contribution—not only is it highly entertaining in itself but it also serves as a terrific analogy for recent results
in the commercial space insurance industry (however hard we've tried,
we still seem to be losing money)."

We never found out if the exploding whale helped turn Janet's
industry around financially, but we do know she used it in a presentation to a group of 150 international aviation insurance underwriters in
Copenhagen, a few of whom later asked for their own copies.

We weren't always sure of the nature of the organizations that wrote
to us. For instance, while a number of local Chambers of Commerce
contacted us from around the country, we also heard from a concern
called "Deitchman and Deitchman, Inc." of Hurst, Texas, whose letter-
head proclaimed it to be "Your Chamber Connection."

"I would like to make it [the whale], available to any U.S. Chamber
of Commerce that asks about it." wrote Macy Deitchman. We thought
that was a good idea, because it might serve to reduce the number of
inquiries sent to us.

———

Of the four major categories of requests we saw develop—government, education, business, and media—requests from the latter were of
the least interest to me. Call it jealousy or professional pride, but I was not
at all interested in the many programs that wanted to make *our* unique
story *theirs*. It wasn't a matter of exclusivity; countless other journalists
had written about the whale and the video in a variety of places.

But there was something about other broadcasters asking for their
own copies. "Go find your own weird stuff," seemed to be the admittedly ungracious feeling somewhere deep in my heart. And it was worse
when a few organizations actually *paid* to broadcast the exploding whale
story, that money going not to us but to the television station that
employed us and owned the rights to our story.

(Several years ago, Doug suggested that we pool our resources and
buy the rights to the story from KATU for, say, $5,000. He thought the

company would go for it since the exploding whale had already been pirated by scores of Web sites. I thought it a dumb idea and begged off, only to have the station sell the rights for a one-time use of the story to a program for $15,000 only a month or two later.)

Doug and I were also amused that a variety of programs unabashedly asked if they could use our stuff, free of charge.

We heard from the *Jeopardy* quiz show ("We are doing a question about the whale that was blown up . . ."); *The Daily Show* ("We would love to license your legendary whale removal and explosion footage"); and from *Real TV* (". . . I hope KATU-TV will agree to license the archival footage of the 1966 [?] beached whale removal"). On the last count, I strongly felt that we shouldn't have to share the story with any outfit that didn't even bother to get the year of the incident right.

But my animosity toward other broadcasters trying to pirate our story was occasionally softened by correspondents who were thoughtful or conniving enough to be complimentary of our work.

"The 'Whale Story' is one of the funniest news stories I've ever seen," wrote David Berrent, executive producer of *Network Event Theatre*, getting my immediate attention.

"Apparently," he explained, "the tape has been circulating newsrooms, production companies, and advertising agencies all over New York. The copy that I have is a twentieth-generation dub on VHS, and I would love to find the original. . . ." Of course he received it, straightaway.

International media organizations also sent us their requests, with the Germans leading the field in terms of numbers.

"My name is Darrin," wrote one, "& I work for a German television show called *Caught On Tape* (COT). I'm looking for a piece of footage that I believe you may have. In it a whale that has died on the beach is blown up spraying remains on all the fleeing spectators." I actually liked it when correspondents explained our story to us, it being somehow refreshing to see how others described the incident.

But our favorite international media request came from Television New Zealand.

Their representative wrote to explain that the network was working on "a thirteen-part series with the working title *Unnatural Histories*." It was apparently a coproduction with Animal Planet on the Discovery Channel.

Julie Watson's letter for TVNZ contained an interesting bit of information we had never heard of before.

"We understand you did a news item about a dead whale which was dynamited," she explained. "We have footage of a similar incident shot in 1937, from Archive Films New York, but we would like to see your more recent news story." Someday, Doug and I agreed, we must write the people at Animal Planet for a copy of *their* exploding whale!

Surprisingly, there was one group of broadcasters I always expected to hear from but never did—the national radio talk show hosts. We would occasionally hear from local radio people, usually at those times that we were broadcasting our own "anniversary" stories of the exploding whale, but none from outside of Portland.

There was one exception. A photographer on our staff who was a fan of the late-night talk show hosted by Art Bell couldn't wait to tell me that the exploding whale had become a recurring topic at one point years ago. He even called the program to report that he worked with the reporter who actually covered the story, but Art Bell seemed more interested in playing detective for a few nights, trying to determine "the validity of this bizarre story," rather than ending the speculation by talking to a direct source.

"You have to call into the program yourself," my photographer friend implored enthusiastically, but I never did. That would only bring more dub requests.

Finally, I think the most creative use of the exploding whale by another television program was the work of producers who didn't even contact us for a copy of the video.

In 1999, an episode of CBS's *Family Law* contained a subplot about a state highway official who had the responsibility of removing a dead whale from a beach. You can surmise the rest—dynamite is used to blow up the whale, and a piece of blubber hits a guy who inevitably decides to sue the state. It was our story, no doubt, and I loved the idea that it made a dramatic series, but not everyone was as thrilled.

"This subplot was 'ripped from the headlines' of a *ShopTalk* story a few years back," charged the online media newsletter. Doug and I were greatly amused that someone else felt "their" story had been pirated.

———

I believe it's fair to say that most of the people who contacted us and made some reasonable explanation for wanting their own copy of the exploding whale ultimately received one, though not necessarily directly from us. As it became increasingly more available from a variety of Web sites, and because the quality of our copy was not much better than what could be downloaded from the Internet, that's where Doug referred many of our correspondents.

"At the beginning," Doug explained, "if I felt folks were going to use it for their own private showing and not for distribution or profit, we would send them a copy as a courtesy. But a number of them, I referred to the Internet."

However, it's also true that some of the more wordy requests, the ones full of bureaucratic jargon and going to great lengths to explain "official" reasons for requesting a dub, rankled Doug for a time. During this period, I happen to know that he refused to send anyone a copy unless there was a frank admission that the correspondent also thought it would be funny to see a whale blow up.

One letter from a U.S. Army Corps of Engineers hydrologist hit just the right tone. "I would like to see this action merely out of curiosity," wrote Dr. Charles Belin. "I would like the tape for personal use." Doug liked the direct, honest approach and waived the humor requirement in this case.

I couldn't blame him for growing weary of wading through paragraph after paragraph of explanations about why Major So and So or Dr. Whatsitt needed the video for his conference. Besides being the guy who had to make the dubs, package them up and send them out, in his heart, Doug knew full well there was only one real reason anyone wanted a copy of the story.

"They . . . just . . . want . . . to . . . see . . . a . . . whale . . . blow . . . up," I heard Doug say in a monotone on more than one occasion. He made the same, well-measured comment in the story KGO reporter Wayne Freedman produced for his San Francisco television audience.

However, even given that understanding, as Doug and I over the years would discuss whatever organization had most recently contacted us and mull yet again how word had spread about this insignificant, solitary event, we never fully understood the apparent global interest.

"I still don't get it," Doug said recently. "It's an interesting piece, but I'm befuddled by the idea that it's of interest to so many folks. They jam up Web sites, they call strangers, you and me, and ask for copies of it. And the quality is so poor—I mean it's an explosion, that's all. I don't get it."

Even so, there was one inquiry, only a few years back, which still haunts me personally.

I received a call from a school security official in Colorado who wanted a copy of our story, and I must admit I was only paying scant attention as he made the usual explanation that the video would be used for training purposes, to show that school officers needed to be reminded that anything could happen at any time, and they needed to be ready for it. I simply waited for the caller to make his point before transferring him to Doug's extension, which is what I routinely did with such calls.

But the security officer added something that instantly shook me.

"Mr. Linnman," he said, "we're the Columbine School District, and we take these matters very seriously."

After forwarding his call to Doug, I thought for a long time about what he had said. Why in the world, I wondered, would a school district which had faced the very worst reality—a shooting that resulted in the untimely deaths of innocent students and teachers—need our video to remind security officers they must be prepared for any eventuality? I thought about the question at length before arriving at a conclusion, which, I suppose, might be rather obvious to others.

Whatever humor might be found in state officials using dynamite to detonate a dead whale, and flattening a man's new car in the process, would be of greater value to the school security people in Colorado than anyone I could think of. They had experienced the worst tragedy imaginable, and if a little levity provided by an exploding whale served to lighten things up a bit as they trained to do their jobs even better, then I couldn't think of a better use for our story.

CHAPTER TWENTY

Giving Kids Their Own Legs

Let me pass, I have to follow them, I am their leader!
—Ledru-Rollin, French politician, 1848

WHEN I VISIT SCHOOLS, kids always want to know about the most embarrassing moment or biggest mistake their basic hometown newscaster ever made on TV. Since their world is filled with potentially embarrassing things and big mistakes made in front of their friends, I guess it's comforting to know that a TV person could do a dumb thing everyone might see. If that's so, I must be America's leading comforter of children, because I've made a satellite truck full of mistakes on the air, all of them pretty dumb.

Most audiences are entertained by blooper stories of all kinds, but student groups in particular seem to enjoy hearing about something that happened to me in the early years when I was a sportscaster. I think they especially like the story because it involves a subject the juvenile mind, and my own, almost always finds humorous—the inopportune passing of gas. At least that's how I tell the story.

One night during the late news I reported a story about the Gold Cup hydroplane races, which were to be held on Lake Washington in Seattle the following weekend. I used a taped interview with well-known racer Bill Muncey, which I had taken off the ABC Network feed. My big mistake was not previewing the story prior to putting it on the air.

The advance information from the network indicated that the story ended with the interview, with the famous driver's final words, or "out-cue," being, "So, it should be a good race on Sunday." With that, the video package would end and we would come back to me live, on camera in the studio, and I'd introduce the next story.

You should know that I have absolutely no understanding of how the electronic or engineering side—the technical stuff—of our business works. The hardworking people who get us on the air and into viewers' homes do their jobs in the same building as I do and many of them are personal friends, but theirs is a completely different world, one which I don't pretend to comprehend.

I do know, however, there can be glitches in what we put on the air—a quick flash of pictures without audio, or a split second of audio without video. When it happens, it's usually when we switch from one thing to another.

As the hydroplane package ended, I popped back onto the screen. But before I was able to say a word, there was a very rude sound that everyone—those watching at home and everyone in our studio—could hear quite clearly. Someone had obviously passed gas, or so it sounded.

What I didn't know about my hydroplane story was that there was some additional footage following the last words of the Muncy interview, simply pictures and wild sound, no narration, of a hydroplane speeding through the water. We never actually saw the hydroplane on the screen, but what we heard was a fraction of a second of a roaring engine. Insert your own sound effect here, but trust me, it sounded like someone was having a major problem, and I was the guy everyone was looking at.

The reaction in the studio was partly predictable; everyone burst into raucous, spontaneous laughter. But there was another reaction I'd never seen before and haven't seen since. The two anchormen on the main news set, the three studio camera operators, and the floor director all fell to their hands and knees on the floor, laughing uncontrollably. Someone would suggest later that they were just trying to find the "clean" air, but the truth was everyone present was responding physically, it was just too funny to remain seated. I'll never forget what the anchors looked like, in suits and ties, having pushed their chairs back from the anchor desk to get down on all fours and have a good belly laugh. (Many these days only wear half a suit—casual pants and running shoes, shorts in the summer, being the norm *underneath* the desk.)

Of course, I was laughing harder than anyone. It was reminiscent of the old Steve Allen sportscaster bit where the great comedian and late-night host, playing his sportscaster character, Biff Barnes, started laughing and couldn't stop. I know what he felt like, and the harder I tried to straighten up, the more impossible it became.

Finally, I managed to squeeze out the words, "We'll be right back after this word from Oly!" the tears streaming down my face. It wasn't time for a commercial from my sponsor at the time, Olympia Beer, but I couldn't think of what else to do. The director, fortunately, picked up my cue and ran the commercial.

Near the end of the sixty-second spot, all of us were back in place and had regained our professional composure. But only seconds before I was cued to be back on the air, the director's voice came out of a studio speaker. "Paul," he said urgently, "do you want to disclaim your error?" Now, I was really confused. "What should I say?" I asked back, "that I didn't fart a minute ago?"

Suddenly everyone was laughing hard once more, down on all fours again, with me live on television and expected to go on with my sports segment. All I could do was join the others and laugh uncontrollably. I figured that in my three-and-a-half-minute sports report that night, I laughed for a full minute-thirty, before referring people to the next day's paper for their sports results, my time having been wasted. All in all, it was not a professional effort—hysterically funny, but not very professional.

I was still laughing when I got back to the newsroom, only to find my boss trying to answer the many phones, which were ringing like crazy. Not surprisingly, many viewers were offended by what they thought I'd done, not to mention my laughing uncontrollably about it, suggesting I should take my little gas problem to a less visible line of work, like grave digging.

"Hey, you started this, fella," said Mr. Hawkins, covering the receiver of a phone he had already answered as he shouted across the room. "Start apologizing to these people who are calling!"

I picked up a phone and punched a line that was blinking only to hear my own wife's voice. "That was so embarrassing," she said. "We can't live here anymore; we have to move." To this day, I don't think Vicki believes for a moment the obnoxious noise she heard that night came from the hydroplane video, but I know it did. And I've never met a group of school kids who didn't love hearing the story. If it somehow makes them feel better about the little things they feel embarrassed about in life, I'm happy to keep telling it.

————

Doing television feature stories, I have met many incredibly charitable people who have come up with much more important and creative ways to help children, especially those with big needs. At the top of the list, I'd put a Portland businessman named Duncan Campbell.

I relate to Duncan, who has also become a friend over the years, because our growing-up years were much alike, and they weren't great. One time Duncan took me around Northeast Portland and showed me all of the taverns he grew up in. His parents were alcoholics, and when his dad wasn't in prison, they would hit one watering hole after another, letting their young son somehow make his own fun for long hours in whatever drinking establishment they happened to frequent that day.

Somehow, Duncan grew up to be an eminently likeable adult, a husky guy who favors V-neck sweaters with button-down shirts and who seems to be perpetually smiling, his dark eyes in constant twinkle mode. To me, Duncan always looks like a hug waiting to happen.

There must be numerous ways that a person can react to parental neglect or a lack of nurturing as a child, or to simply losing out on the carefree joy of just being a kid—most of them negative. At the least, blame can always be placed on Mom or Dad for not providing what was needed for a happy and productive life. Duncan Campbell chose to adopt a more positive attitude.

"I promised myself, if I was successful in life," Duncan told me, "I'd do what I could to keep other kids from having a childhood like mine." Fortunately for hundreds of children in many U.S. cities, Duncan became a very successful businessman, having made a nice living in timber management when Oregon still had plenty of timber to manage. That allowed him to start a unique and remarkably successful program called Friends of the Children.

His idea was to hire professional, adult mentors to befriend the most troubled children, chosen in the first grade as the kids who faced the most impossible challenges academically and socially. Each mentor, or "Friend," is assigned eight children who they spend time with on a regular basis, playing, doing schoolwork, going places, and just being friends.

"The Friends have values, and they share these values with the children," Duncan explained in our first story on his program, "and they are role models. Then the children reflect the behavior of the adults around them."

When I first heard about the concept, something troubled me about paying an adult to befriend a child. Wouldn't volunteers be a better fit, people who did it out of goodness rather than for pay? Duncan explained that while he thought volunteers were wonderful, they couldn't be counted on to provide the consistency required by these very needy kids. Plans change, careers may require a move to another city, a more compelling volunteer job may come along, all things which could remove a volunteer from a child's life, leading to another possible letdown and further feelings of failure and abandonment.

"What we do is real, and it works," Duncan said, "and we're going to have a better community because of it."

Our second television story on Friends of the Children allowed us to follow a Friend named Jenna and her student, Christina. They had been together for six years, and during that time, Jenna went from being a sullen, unhappy seven-year-old to an outgoing, self-assured teenager. The two pulled out scrapbooks and showed me pictures of Jenna as a scowling second-grader, then photos taken in more recent years when she appeared to be loving life, big time.

"Look at how mad you used to be," Jenna laughs in Christina's direction, "and now look, you're laughing and playing."

Christina is quick to agree. "Me and my dad would get in arguments all of the time, so I thought all adults were like that. So I was mostly rude to adults." That's all behind her now.

"She looks forward to the future," Jenna adds. "She has goals that she didn't have before." Which was just what Duncan Campbell was hoping for when he began the program.

"What we're trying to do," he concludes, "is break the cycle of poverty and crime by letting them see that there are options in their lives, and they can make a choice themselves to have a different life."

By all accounts it's working. In 1993, Friends of the Children started with three Friends serving 24 children in one Northeast Portland neighborhood. Today, it employs 36 Friends and reaches 275 youth throughout the city.

Of the program participants, 97 percent passed their grade in school last year, and 98 percent remained enrolled in a regular school program, some in neighborhoods where the dropout rate approaches 70 percent. Of these formerly unreachable, antisocial children, 43 percent participate in extracurricular activities, 4.3 percent made the honor role, and one was elected student body president. Not bad for kids whose first-grade teachers were convinced that they were destined to fail. Many of their friends left school behind long ago, but for some reason, the Friends of the Children group seems to beat the odds.

Furthermore, while many of these children live in neighborhoods where there is gang activity, nearly 98 percent of them have never been incarcerated in a juvenile justice facility, and less than 10 percent have had involvement with gangs, which can be very hard to escape for survival reasons alone. And finally, like Duncan Campbell, 40 percent of them have a father who is or has been incarcerated, and 62 percent are exposed to drug or alcohol abuse in their homes, yet 98 percent of them do not use alcohol on a regular basis.

Friends of the Children now operates out of an old school that Campbell purchased and beautifully renovated (with help from his wife, Cindy, on the friendly and inviting decor). The building serves as the chief gathering place for the kids and their mentors. There's almost always basketball being played in the gym, the well-equipped computer room is in constant use, and the comfortable casual areas are given to long conversations between the children and their Friends.

"We're going to be friends forever," Christina proudly proclaims of Jenna, as the two sit and chat. Both acknowledge that sometimes the communication has been much more urgent. "If there's something going on," Jenna explains, "I've received calls from Christina at midnight, crying, and just needing someone to talk to."

That also seems to be why experts say the program works. A thirty-year veteran of children and family services at both the state and county levels was interviewed for our stories on Campbell's program. "It works," she said, "because the essence is a one-on-one relationship that is sustained over time between an adult professional mentor and child."

That's precisely what Campbell had in mind. "We can only change things one kid at a time, one family at a time, one block at a time, one neighborhood at a time," he said recently. "Things went bad one kid at a time, one family at a time, and that's how we're going to fix it."

However, there is no reason that many cities can't attempt the same approach at the same time, and so the program also has a national office. Programs based on the successful Portland model have now started up in New York City, Washington, D.C., Cincinnati, San Francisco, and a half dozen other cities.

"People ask me why it wasn't done before," muses Campbell. "I guess it's just that someone has to do it for the first time to get it going."

All it took was a little know-how from a guy who had to spend his childhood sitting in taverns.

———————

One of the benefits of a career in journalism—broadcast or print—is the constant variety it brings; the subject matter or frame of reference, especially in television news, often can change by the hour. At about the same time that I came across Duncan Campbell, I met a young woman who was doing equally incredible things with another group of children and who also faced tremendous challenges. All she really did was put them on horseback.

Kerri Knaus and her sister Sue McCarty started a program, which they initially saddled with an impossibly difficult acronym, H.O.R.S.E.S., for Horses Outdoor Recreation Specialized Equipment Services. It continues to thrive and grow today, nearly two decades later, as The Adaptive Riding Institute, but most folks still call it, simply, HORSES.

While Sue is able-bodied, Kerri has a slow, progressive form of muscular dystrophy, which required her to use a wheelchair but didn't impair her creative thinking at all. She never met anyone who she didn't think would be better off on a horse, especially the physically challenged.

"The horse," she told me, "gives those individuals like myself an extra pair of legs that suddenly not only walk, but can run, jump, climb, and do all kinds of things."

Kerri and Sue headquartered their riding facility at a small ranch in the foothills of the Cascade Mountains near Scotts Mills, Oregon. We paid a visit there and met six-year-old Nathaniel, a cute kid with cerebral palsy, who was just learning to ride using specially adapted equipment.

"I'm sure he'll be able to get on a horse and ride, because he has his future ahead of him and lots of time to practice," Kerri explained.

Then she introduced us to eight-year-old Bobby, already a veteran rider of two years. Bobby wore a protective helmet beneath a huge, black cowboy hat, and told us he was looking forward to his next wilderness ride.

"There's this mountain she showed me," Bobby beamed, "and I think it would be fun to ride over it."

We watched many young riders, nervous at first, but then clearly thrilled as the big, well-trained animals started to move under them. You could see the recognition in their eyes as bodies that had previously been unable to propel themselves were suddenly given the power to move, in any direction and at any speed.

But Kerri was quick to point out that her program was not about exercise, nor was it about therapy. This horseback riding was for recreation and the sheer joy of it.

"If you don't get any physical benefit from that, that's fine," she said. "We're out here to have fun, to see the woods, to be in a sunny wilderness area, not for therapy, not for exercise." Even so, most experts are in agreement that riding does serve therapeutic and exercise purposes, as well.

As the riders became more proficient, and with the help of expert volunteers, they'd take their mounts on overnighters and weekend trips to some of the most beautiful wilderness areas in the Pacific Northwest—to the high desert, the beach, the mountains. These were activities, according to the HORSES brochure, that "focus on the limitless, not on limitations."

HORSES is now the oldest disabled riding program in Oregon, providing equestrian opportunities to people of all ages. It also helps develop custom-made adaptive riding equipment, and rehabilitates horses suffering from injury. In summers, in Silver Falls State Park near Salem, HORSES operates the first-ever disability-friendly public horse rental. People from around the world, both the disabled and able-bodied, come to Oregon's largest state park to enjoy the guided trail rides. The program begun by two sisters is now considered the model for other organizations looking to start their own barrier-free recreational riding programs, throughout the United States and internationally.

And to think it all happened because of a very simple idea: Why not give a person a way to trade in two useless legs for four strong ones? Hundreds of riders make the discovery every year.

"I've done it so long," says Kerri, "it just seems normal, and sometimes you forget the magic of it. But then a new rider comes along and you see the revelation and excitement in their eyes, and you realize it is unique—a special feeling you can't get anywhere else."

It's hard for those of us who aren't physically challenged to imagine not being able to walk at all for years, and then, suddenly, the vast wilderness lies before you and you're free to pick a direction and just go—at top speed, if you like! What a thrill it must be—something that Kerri and Sue knew all along, they just found a way to share it.

———

It seems we report nightly on the evening news about another expensive new program the federal government is launching to help some group of citizens whose needs are not being met. If we throw enough money at a problem, the theory seems to go, everything will be all right. But still, those with physical or other special challenges must constantly struggle to keep up with the rest of society, no matter how many new programs are created.

On still another front, we as a society seem to be paying quite a premium to imprison countless offenders who, it might be argued, were somehow deprived at an early age of having their needs met. Perhaps these are adults who started life like some of the kids in Duncan Campbell's program, but who didn't benefit from the personal attention of a role model. In either case, it seems like taxpayers are spending a lot of their hard-earned dollars on problems that could have been addressed long ago in much simpler ways.

After more than three decades of meeting people like Campbell and Kerri Knaus—innovators who see a problem and have the vision and the initiative to fix it—I'm convinced that most of society's problems are better solved by creative, giving individuals than by government programs or penitentiaries.

If others don't have the same perspective, perhaps it's because our evening newscasts don't spend much time telling us about the people who know the importance of giving a kid a friend, or a ride on a horse.

CHAPTER TWENTY-ONE

The Two Who Blew

It's the place where my prediction from the sixties finally came true: 'In the future everyone will be famous for fifteen minutes.' I'm bored with that line. I never use it anymore. My new line is, 'In fifteen minutes, everybody will be famous.'

—Andy Warhol, 1979

HAVING THOUGHT ABOUT IT for all of these years, I'm reasonably sure the exploding whale would have been forgotten long ago had it not been for two things: George Thornton's disposal plan didn't go quite as he'd hoped, and Walter Umenhofer's car got crushed.

Thornton thought his explosion would pulverize the whale, leaving only bite-size pieces for the gulls. Had that happened, the scavengers would have been fat and happy, and the story would have been over. Indeed, the explosion is fun to watch, but only once or twice; as previously noted, it looks no different than the thousands of other explosions we've all seen in the movies.

Its the aftermath that puts one to thinking about the strangeness of the entire mess, and the scenes of Umenhofer's flattened Oldsmobile are what evoke the greatest response. "What an unlucky schmuck," is a logical first reaction; "thank God it wasn't my car," is the illogical second. (I've heard people express the latter who weren't within two hundred miles of the explosion that day—some of them weren't even born yet!)

But the plan didn't work, the car got blubberized, and an urban legend was born. (The exploding whale story is often categorized, on the Internet and elsewhere, as an "urban legend," a misnomer if I've ever heard one. The most curious explanation for this that I've read came from William Boei, then a staff writer for the *Vancouver Sun* in British Columbia. "The exploding whale qualifies as an urban legend," Boei explained in an article in 1998, because it's "a story so compelling we have to tell someone else about it." Uh, okay.)

———

In 1995, at the time of the twenty-fifth anniversary of the incident, Doug Brazil and I returned to Florence to produce an historical series on the subject for the same station that broadcast the original story. Doug had risen through the ranks to become one of our newsroom administrators and no longer took pictures, so a Channel 2 photographer followed the two of us as we returned to the blast site and then traipsed around the nearby town.

We spent considerable time talking to local residents, fishermen, shop owners, people at the newspaper, and others about what they did and didn't remember about the now-infamous incident of a quarter century past, and how it impacted their town. Interestingly, we found many residents who hadn't even heard the story; these were mostly former Californians who'd migrated to Oregon recently to live the good life, many of them opening shops in Florence's old town. We also found a few longtime residents who not only remembered the exploding whale but who were still embarrassed by the old story, suggesting that it had put their town on the world map for the wrong reasons.

Still others had concocted their own versions of the incident. "It was a case of a little too much cure—something like a minor atomic bomb going off," a fisherman told us.

And, remarkably, while our return to the South Coast resulted in a weeklong series for the news, we didn't even visit the two most important and obvious players in our original story: George Thornton and Walter Umenhofer.

The truth is, I haven't interviewed Thornton since the day of the explosion in 1970, and I've never even met Umenhofer. Now, how in the world can a man who calls himself a reporter explain that?

————————

Since I first met George Thornton on the day of the incident in 1970, I've had a soft spot in my heart for this career government worker. First, he was kind to me, granting me an interview and responding earnestly to what may have seemed naive questions while he was in the middle of dealing with a perplexing problem. Furthermore, I've always felt bad that our video may have suggested to viewers worldwide that Thornton was a colossal boob who had done an incredibly stupid thing by trying to dynamite an eight-ton whale. That was certainly never my own conclusion.

And while we've never talked about it in any detail since, I have studied the explanations Thornton has given to others regarding his day of infamy.

"I can remember it vividly," Thornton told Ed Schoaps for his ODOT newsletter story.

"I got designated because district engineer Dale Allen and others took off hunting when this thing broke—conveniently, I think." Schoaps wrote that Thornton himself laughed at this thought, then added: "To be fair, they had planned on going, but this thing made them all the more anxious to go."

And so Thornton, then assistant district highway engineer, was left holding the bag, or blubber, to be accurate, but bore no apparent grudge against his colleagues for it. You've got to like him for that. But was it his call to use the explosives, and how was such a questionable decision arrived at?

The answers can be found in a *Sports Illustrated* article written by Ed Christopherson for the magazine's "Yesterday" section in October

1974. (By the way, this is the single best piece of writing I've ever read on the incident, and there have been hundreds.) Christopherson outlines Thornton's efforts and ultimate options in detail:

> *Thornton phoned other coastal highway divisions, the Coast Guard, the health department; police, pollution-control authorities, ecologists, explosive experts, et al. His options seemed to include burning, burying, and towing the carcass elsewhere. He rejected burning, because first he'd have to move it so the stench wouldn't carry to Florence, and because attempts to burn dead whales had not proven successful. Burying works in the case of sea lions and smaller whales, but this one was so near the water that the next tide would wash it out. Towing? The whale was by now ripe enough to be falling apart. "Otherwise we might have pulled it up to the dunes, where we could have buried it," Thornton says.*
>
> *All in all, it is not surprising that a department that deals in concrete and steel and rock and machinery would end up choosing explosives. "We figured if we could disintegrate it enough—get it into small enough pieces—the crabs and seagulls would clean it up in a short time," Thornton recalls.*

We can therefore conclude that the decision was not a hasty one, and that all options were taken into consideration. What's more, there was another expert source, not mentioned in the Christopherson story, that Thornton consulted before the blast. No less than the United States Department of the Navy concurred with his ultimate decision to use explosives.

So why didn't it work out as expected? Why wasn't the whale pulverized into pieces small enough to be consumed by scavengers?

Larry Bacon, another good reporter who was actually present at the explosion, covering his first front-page story for Eugene, Oregon's highly regarded *Register-Guard* newspaper, talked to Thornton afterward. Bacon recalls that Thornton appeared calm when talking about it, and as Bacon later wrote, "even tried to put a positive spin on things."

"It went just exactly right," Bacon quoted Thornton, "except the blast funneled a hole in the sand under the whale." His conclusion was that the hole served to misdirect the blast, thereby diminishing its effectiveness.

As to any final thoughts Thornton may have had about what had happened that day, Christopherson addresses in the form of a question: "Would Thornton use dynamite to get rid of a whale again?"

"It depends on the location," he says carefully. "We've had some correspondence with a naval explosive expert who said we should have used twice as much dynamite. This would have more or less vaporized the whale."

Thornton also offered a rather good-natured conclusion for Ed Schoaps' story.

"I said to my supervisors, usually when something happens like this, the person ends up getting promoted," he said. "Sure enough, about six months later, I got promoted to Medford."

———

At the time that we produced our twenty-fifth anniversary series on the exploding whale, I thought it would be convenient to travel from Florence east to Medford, where Thornton had retired in 1990, for a look-back interview.

But when I called him to make arrangements, I immediately sensed that George Thornton was most aware of how viewers around the globe had been chuckling at our exploding whale video for a quarter of a century, and that he didn't appreciate it at all.

I understood, and suggested in our telephone conversation that this would be his chance to tell his side of the story. Unfortunately, my wording could not have been worse.

When he seemed reluctant, I appealed: "But Mr. Thornton, don't you want to have a chance to explain what went wrong?"

There was a momentary silence, and then I heard Thornton's voice, quieter than it had been before: "What do you mean, 'what went wrong?'" he asked in a monotone.

I knew at that moment that there wasn't a way in the world I'd get my interview. I thanked Mr. Thornton and hung up, deflated. A professional journalist for twenty-seven years and I was still making mistakes that might be considered on a par with dynamiting whales.

More recently, feeling that I must speak to Thornton for this book, I came up with what I thought was a stroke of genius for getting an interview: I'd ask his former colleague in the transportation department, Ed Schoaps, to make the request on my behalf.

Ed agreed, but held out little hope, reminding me that while Thornton had consented to an interview for Schoaps's article in 1994, he had declined subsequent requests.

"No more, I'm not interested in talking to reporters about this,'" Schoaps quoted Thornton as having said. "I think his actual words were, 'I'm a little tired of the whale.'"

Nonetheless, the highway division's top public affairs man made the request for me. Several days later, to my regret, Schoaps e-mailed me that Thornton had declined, apparently still rankled by the subject thirty-three years later, and thirteen years after his retirement.

The suggestion that it would be his chance to set the record straight didn't help either, and Thornton's final answer was both priceless and ironic.

He told Schoaps that whenever he has talked to a reporter about the whale, the facts get "all blown out of proportion."

"I'm sure he did not intend the pun," Ed explained, "but there it was."

My own conclusion is that George Thornton is a decent guy who, based on his experience and all other factors on that day in 1970, did his level best to do the job right. It's a popular pastime in this country to joke about government blunders and to poke fun at bumbling bureaucrats, but in this case I don't believe there were major errors in judgment.

Thornton acknowledged at the time that he couldn't be certain of how much dynamite to use. In retrospect, perhaps he should have moved all of us who were present, and our cars, farther away, but I would have strenuously complained about that, since we had a job to do, too.

For whatever part the wide distribution of our original story has played in making George Thornton look like an inept public servant, I am truly sorry; that was never our intention, and I believe our script bears that out. Plus, we thought the story was over and done with at the time, and had no intention of taking it any further.

My take on the entire episode, to paraphrase a contemporary expression, is that blubber happens. And if I were George Thornton, I wouldn't want to talk to me about it either.

Walter Umenhofer is another story. From what I can tell, he has never been reluctant to talk with reporters about getting his Oldsmobile wiped out, and I fully intended to catch up with him for an interview for our 1995 series. But something happened that made it unnecessary.

Wayne Freedman, a celebrated feature reporter for KGO, ABC's affiliate station in San Francisco, had somehow gotten wind of the exploding whale story about the same time that we were producing our twenty-fifth anniversary stories. (I've scooped other reporters on stories before, but am particularly proud of beating Wayne, who I consider a friend, by a quarter century!)

In the fall of 1995, Wayne's station dispatched him to Oregon to retell the story for the Bay Area audience, and this resulted in his interviewing most of the players, including Doug Brazil and me. (I was embarrassed later when I saw Wayne's story and realized that I was a horrible interview subject—a slow talker with weird personal mannerisms!)

George Thornton, I was relieved to hear, had also declined Wayne's interview request, but Walter Umenhofer was a willing participant. When Wayne offered to share sound bites from his interview with Umenhofer, I happily accepted, saving myself and the crew a trip to

Springfield, Oregon. That may have been the lazy way out, but when you're under the gun to produce a multipart series airing on several newscasts over several days, all shortcuts are welcome.

And so I still haven't met Mr. Umenofer, but would like to. He appears to be a garrulous, fun-loving guy who's quick to laugh and who enjoys telling a good story. Somewhere in his sixties, with thinning, gray hair, Umenhofer was interviewed in his own easy chair for Wayne's story, his television remote control nearby, but I could also picture this likeable man sitting in countless bars or coffee shops, retelling his incredible story of years ago.

I learned from Freedman's interview that Walter Umenhofer, who had demolition experience in the military, actually spoke to George Thornton on that day in 1970, telling him that he was using too much dynamite. Thornton didn't buy it.

"But the guy says, 'Anyway, I'm going to have everyone on top of those dunes far away,'" Umenhofer said, quoting the assistant highway engineer. "And I says, yeah, and I'm going to be the furtherest SOB down that way."

At the time, Umenhofer was an executive with the Kingsford charcoal briquette company, and he had made the trip from the Springfield–Eugene area to surreptitiously look at property in Florence for a new plant. When he was told that a port authority official he wished to speak to could be found at the whale site, Umenhofer drove out South Jetty Road along with three others—his fourteen-year-old son, a county pollution control executive, and a real estate agent. He parked his new Oldsmobile in the third turnout before making his way to the beach, where he took in the scene, and decided to move well away for the blast. He watched it all happen.

"And they touched that sucker off, let me tell you," Umenhofer recalls with great enthusiasm in the Freedman interview. "That thing went off, and it was the biggest mushroom cloud you've ever seen. And it was red and white and black, and it was nothing but guts and blood and gunk."

Umenhofer remembered accurately that it took a little while before bystanders nearby realized that the mist and larger remnants of the whale were coming their way.

"And I'm just watching this one piece," Umenhofer says, warming to the story. "There's a big piece up there, it's kind of flubbering and floating around. And it just suddenly stopped, and it came flat down and . . . KA-POW!" Umenhofer laughs hard, as if he is hearing the account for the first time.

Another version of the story, the one in *Sports Illustrated*, has someone nearby saying to Umenhofer, "You're lucky that's not your car."

"My God! It *is* my car!," Umenhofer is said to have hollered back.

It was a green Oldsmobile Regency with a black vinyl top, and its roof had taken a left-rear corner hit. A chunk of blubber about three feet by three feet crushed the roof to the seats, blowing shattered glass in a sixty-foot radius. Remarkably, no one was injured, and officials estimated that the blubber projectile had traveled a good 450 yards from the blast site.

"It was a neat car, I'd just gotten it," Umenhofer explained. "The funny thing was the dealer's slogan where I bought it, Dunham's Olds-Cadillac in Eugene—it was get a 'Whale of a Deal.' Yeah, I got a helluva a whale of a deal," Umenhofer concludes, laughing harder than before.

When Ed Schoaps of the Oregon Highway Department wrote his account of the incident years later, his story began with Walter Umenhofer stating, "My insurance company is never going to believe this." I don't doubt the validity of the quote, but the whale–Oldsmobile collision was never an issue for Umenhofer's insurance agent. Within days of the mishap, Walter received a check from the state of Oregon for the full retail value of his car.

Needless to say, his confidential trip to look at South Coast real estate received a great deal of attention, and has continued to do so over the years. He's been seen on television numerous times, was interviewed on national talk radio, and was still surprised to welcome the television crew from San Francisco twenty-five years later.

And he still thinks, with everyone else who hears it, that his is a funny story.

"What makes it funny," he told the *Register Guard*'s Larry Bacon, "is nobody got hurt."

I still maintain that, had the whale been vaporized as had been hoped for, and had that smelly piece of whale meat missed the Oldsmobile, the story would have died long ago. George Thornton would have retired without notice, Walter Umenhofer would have one less story to tell, Wayne Freedman would have stayed in San Francisco, and you wouldn't be reading this book. Who could have seen it all coming?

But let the record show that there were at least two on the beach that day in 1970 who may have had a slight idea that a disaster was in the making. Besides the state workers, they were the only two who, from past experience, knew something about explosives and their potential effect. When George Thornton ordered everyone present to move a quarter of a mile away, Walter Umenhofer and Bruce Mate, the young marine biologist, went twice as far, placing themselves a half mile to the south, out of harm's way. Fortunately for Mate, he took his car with him.

CHAPTER TWENTY-TWO

What We Can Learn from Mammals

All of us are watchers—of television, of time clocks, of traffic on the freeway—but few are observers. Everyone is looking, but not many are seeing.

—*Peter M. Leschak*

THE THING I ENJOY MOST about being a reporter is the opportunity it affords to come alongside interesting people and, if but for a moment, get into their lives and into their heads.

How would you like it? Imagine that when you hear about someone in your town who is up to something you find wonderful or fascinating, or perhaps even perplexing, you're able to pick up the telephone and call them. Within a day or two you meet them and ask any question about why they're doing whatever they do, how it started, and what they get from it. No matter what you discover in the exchange, you're guaranteed to go away knowing something you didn't know before.

But then the best part comes—you can create your own story about whoever you met, and share their insight with everyone else. Who knows what might follow? Your story and your feature subject may inspire someone else to do something that's wonderful or fascinating.

It is pure fun, which is the first test of a good job, and the competent feature reporter will never run out of subjects. I have been blessed to meet and report on thousands of them, and still, every day, I find out about others I'd like to catch up with. What's more, the guarantee is still good—I've never met a story subject who didn't teach me something worthwhile.

———

Two sisters on the Oregon Coast, Adaline and Leila Svenson, taught me a new way to experience history. When their father, an old-time blacksmith, passed away, they shut the door on his warehouse-sized shop, leaving it just as it was. Decades later, they invited strangers to drop in and see what such a place looked like in the 1930s and 1940s, a real-life museum as it were, their father's hat and coat and National Recovery Act posters still on the wall, the old potbelly stove ready for duty in the middle of the room, where locals used to gather to talk sports and politics. Visiting that old place in Astoria was not like going to a museum, it was like stepping back in time.

Joe Loprinzi taught me the importance of following through on one's beliefs. When he started his exercise and fitness show on television in the 1950s, everyone thought he was a nut. Of course, now the whole world exercises, and realizes that Joe, a contemporary and friend of Jack LaLanne, was a visionary. He spent his entire working career (mostly at Portland's vulnerable Multnomah Athletic Club), convincing thousands of people that it's never too late to get fit, simply because he believed it with all of his heart, and in those early days didn't mind being called a nut.

In Tillamook, on Oregon's North Coast, Mildred Davey is well into her nineties but still hosts a very good talk show every day on KTIL radio. I learned from Mildred that if you truly love what you do, you don't have to stop doing it until you want to.

It turned out that many others knew that, too. Celia Davis, a 90-year-old jazz singer, Laura Foote, a 103-year-old nurse, Anna Kottcamp, who finally earned her high school diploma at the age of 83, and scores of other oldsters showed me repeatedly that the only thing that can slow you down is you.

When I met Liz Downing, she was a world biathlon champion who virtually no one could beat. Surprisingly, Liz told me she was only an average athlete in high school and college, but had simply discovered two sports (cycling and running) that she could do together better than anyone else. From Liz, I learned that we can all be great at something, it's just a matter of finding the right combination. (No, I haven't discovered my two sports yet, but I'm working on it.)

Dan Barker taught me the value of being a servant. This Vietnam veteran came back from the war with a burning desire to serve others, and did so by planting hundreds of raised vegetable gardens for the elderly poor. Each year, after planting their gardens, he would show the grateful seniors how to harvest their vegetables. Dan financed his efforts by obtaining small grants, and I don't believe I ever met anyone who was more content in his work.

Dale Etna Powers was among the many who taught me that dreams don't have to die. She loved to ride horses and was a guide at a local stable, despite being well into her eighties. Dale's dream, however, was to put on a fine outfit and ride in Portland's Rose Festival Parade, which she ultimately did at the age of ninety-five. In fact, Dale was still riding in the parade at one hundred.

Squid, the police horse, taught me that when one door closes another usually opens. Late in his career on the streets of Portland, Squid became a little spooked. Mud puddles, of all things, began to freak him out—not a good thing for a police horse in a town where it rains a lot. He was retired to a therapeutic riding stable and as far as I know, is still happily giving rides to thrilled youngsters who've never been on a horse before.

Joe Rowan showed me how to take something you love and share it with others. Joe was passionate about water skiing, up early and on the water every morning before work, and back out in the evening doing the same thing. Joe figured that there was no reason blind people couldn't do what he loved to do, and he spent many days in the summers teaching them how. It was a joy to watch.

I couldn't begin to count the number of physically challenged people who taught me that they could do whatever they set their minds to. At the top of this list, I'd put John Rinehart, a disabled cyclist, John Brewer, a paraplegic race car driver, and Rhondee Bariault, a deaf actress and dancer. Bruce Brennan would make the list, too. He was deaf and wanted to be a pilot, but was discouraged by many who said his inability to communicate with ground control towers wouldn't allow it. Bruce took lessons, learned to fly, and landed his plane at small airfields where there aren't any towers to communicate with. The word "handicap" didn't mean a thing to any of these people.

And there were the many who showed me the value of putting your own life on hold to go somewhere in the world where someone needs your help. Matt Starkenburg quit his job, sold his home and all of his possessions, and relocated to Romania where he worked to establish that country's first privately operated orphanage. Drs. Travis and Phyllis Cavens, physicians from Washington state, and Marie Davis, a nurse from Dallas, Oregon, most likely couldn't count the number of devastated countries they've visited to care for the sick and poor, and at their own expense. They're still virtually on-call as volunteers for Northwest Medical Teams, with Marie frequently taking one of her own children along on these vital missions of mercy, to learn the importance of being there for someone in need.

At Camp UKANDU near Rockaway, Oregon, I learned that even kids with the most serious types of cancer can escape their hospitals and clinics for a week of summertime fun. All it takes each year is about a hundred volunteers and medical people, waiting in the wings to administer medication and care as needed. None of these people is paid, but gladly give up their own vacations to make sure that some very ill children are not deprived of one of the great joys of childhood—summer camp. The volunteers want only one thing for their campers each year, that they have an outrageously good time, and they do. Just about every one of these kids will tell you it's the best week of their entire life.

And finally, from Carole Staady and her Phame Academy in Portland, I learned that if you want to take to the stage and sing and dance and act, go for it. The developmentally disabled theater company that Carole founded and directs in Portland puts on the most remarkable productions, because that's what its members love to do. Their audiences seem to love it, too.

––––––––––

I've had the opportunity to report on many more such people—almost all of whom, by the way, didn't really want the attention—but you get the point. There are few jobs that allow you to connect with the most inspirational and creative people imaginable, day in and day out. If journalism is a ticket to discover the world, feature reporting is an invitation to meet its most interesting people, and I'm thankful to have met more than my share.

Which brings us to the question—what was inspirational about the exploding whale, and what did I learn from that?

The honest answer is—nothing major, but a tidbit here and there. When Doug Brazil and I encountered this deadly subject, it was in the early stages of our careers, and we were covering hard news, chasing the lead stories. I'm afraid the guarantee that every story is a learning experience doesn't necessarily apply to those stories that make the biggest headlines.

Still, as I've discussed in earlier chapters, there are small lessons to be found in what happened on the South Coast that day—that life and work don't always go as planned, that one must always be prepared for the unexpected, and that taking a whale blubber shower stinks something awful. These are good things to know, though perhaps can't be considered major life lessons.

But it's also true that the exploding whale ultimately did lead me to some other interesting people, many of whom believed that the story was very educational for them and their associates. So, while I may not have personally picked up a major life lesson from the whale, others who heard about the story did, and after all, the primary role of the journalist is to inform his audience, not himself!

A few others, who didn't look to the whale for learning purposes at all, had some very unusual stories of their own to tell as a result of the incident. They've been writing and calling me since 1970, and over the years I've told many of their stories on television, too.

Perhaps the weirdest call was from a massage therapist from McMinnville, Oregon, who contacted me a quarter century after the fateful explosion to say he had a special memento for me from the whale. With photographer in tow, I paid David Banks a visit, and heard the strangest story yet concerning the incident.

David explained that his grandfather had been a missionary in Africa, and had brought him elephant tusks when he was a child. That apparently gave him the idea, upon hearing of the dead whale on the beach in Florence, of retrieving a few sperm whale teeth, which he did.

With considerable charm and enthusiasm, he told me the story of how he pulled it off, as if he was recounting a wonderful day of agate hunting. But David had actually cut three teeth by hand from the back of the deceased whale's mouth, a grisly endeavor if ever I heard of one.

"It was sickening," David cheerfully agreed. "It took me not quite an hour to get them out of there because I'd have to go in and out for fresh air."

He later cut the teeth into pieces and polished them up, also like agates, creating what I had to admit was a handsome necklace and bracelet for his wife.

"I get more comments on them," Mrs. Banks told us, "because they're originals, you know."

No doubt. And I was given an original, too, though not a piece of jewelry. David gave me a small, polished piece of whale tooth, which he presented as if it was the rarest of gems.

"One guy called me 'the whale dentist,'" he chuckled proudly.

Frankly, I was most pleased to receive this small token of an event that had so influenced my career as a journalist. I still carry the thing around from time to time, like a talisman, and it was in my pocket when I presented the idea for this book to its publishers.

While countless schools have studied the whale story, we found perhaps the best educational use of the exploding whale at Meadow Park Middle School in Beaverton, the Portland suburb that is also home to Oregon's only Fortune 500 company, Nike.

A teacher, Andy Whiten, thought I might like to see how he used the whale annually in his physics class for problem solving, so we paid his classroom a visit.

"I mean, it's a beautiful problem," Andy explained, "how *do* you get an eight-ton whale off the beach?"

His students obviously enjoyed watching the video, and I asked a couple of them what they thought.

"People do some pretty stupid things at times," said one girl.

"I think they could have figured out a better way," said another. "Like I had ten different ideas."

What I really wanted to know from Andy was where he got his copy of the video, and it turned out, his principal provided it. So I put the same question to her.

"I was at another school where the new principal came in and used it in our staff orientation," explained the administrator, and she obtained her copy for the same purpose. "Just as a way to say I didn't plan on blowing up any whales," she said, "that we had a great school, and we'd do problem solving together."

Before I left Meadow Park, the principal also told me that a visiting teacher on an exchange program from Australia had taken a copy home the previous year, and that it was now likely being used in educational systems Down Under.

For the simple fun and creativity of it, I would say that my favorite use of the whale story was brought to my attention by a film animator in New York City.

Daniel Kanemoto wrote to me when he was an undergraduate student at NYU's film school, where he was producing his own animated films. He had downloaded a copy of the exploding whale from the Internet and was oddly captivated by it.

"I found myself completely delighted," he said. "The strangeness of it all—it really inspired me."

While finishing work on his thesis film, a two-year project which was a serious drama about World War I, Daniel decided to relax by working on a second short, the subject of which was, well, you know.

Using the sound track from our story, he animated every scene from the original news account, and in two weeks produced a second film, which he titled *Whalesong*. He had actually written me to inquire about obtaining permission to distribute his new movie, a copy of which he sent us shortly thereafter.

Doug Brazil and I viewed it together and couldn't believe what we saw; it was an incredible piece of work. The very same story we had produced and seen so many times now had me as a cartoon figure, and Doug's photography had been magically transformed into animated scenes, colored in deep blues and blood oranges. We liked it a lot and others apparently did too. A label on the box it came in proclaimed it to be the winner of MTV's animated short contest.

While *Whalesong* was never distributed, Daniel's thesis film, *A Letter from the Western Front*, won awards and received much attention at various film festivals. He works today as a freelance animator in New York, and has fond memories of how the exploding whale helped him unwind in the stressful years when he learned his craft and produced his first work.

"And even after all of these years," Daniel wrote me recently, "I still use the 'exploding whale' shot in the reel I use as a professional animator."

Some day I should tell Daniel Kanemoto that on those occasions when I need to view the exploding whale story, I watch his version instead of mine.

At some point I decided that I should check on some of the "official" uses of the whale, contacting a few of the agencies which wanted their hazmat or bomb disposal guys to better understand the importance of "being prepared for anything," as so many of their letters explained.

At the Oregon State Police Academy in Monmouth, George McCoy, the state fire-training officer, told us that he had been using the video to prove the point to his classes for three years.

"It lets them know," George said, "no matter what kind of an expert you are, you can still make a slight miscalculation."

I observed the cops of the future laugh heartily as they watched the whale blow on video, proving that most of them do have a sense of humor—despite how they appear when writing us tickets.

We also went to Vancouver, Washington, to attend a conference for emergency responders from throughout the Pacific Northwest. These were professionals from emergency relief agencies, hospitals, 911 centers, law enforcement agencies—anyone whose job required them to deal with communities in crisis. The subject of discussion was ominous: the dissemination of public information following the use of a weapon of mass destruction.

Naturally, the exploding whale was a welcome participant, brought to the gathering by Air Force Major Rebecca Colaw, a national expert on handling public information after a catastrophe.

"I've seen the video forty or fifty times now," Major Colaw told me before the meeting, "and I still laugh at it." She said it had been part of her presentations for years, and that she had used it in dozens of conferences from Washington, D.C., to Washington state.

"It shows what happens when you don't consider the ramifications of your actions," said Major Colaw, "and it does it in a funny way. I'll use it forever."

The people at the conference seemed to agree. I sat beside professionals charged with responding to the most tragic incidents, as they laughed at this insignificant one, and concluded that the other sessions across the country in which Major Colaw shared the whale story must have been just like this one. In such a setting, it did make a very good point: that those watching it must be prepared for any eventuality.

Only months later, I found myself wondering about the emergency responders to the terrorist attacks in New York, Washington, D.C., and Pennsylvania. Had they at some earlier time been amused, or perhaps even helped in some small way, by Becky Colaw's presentation? It's possible.

Few reporters ever have the opportunity to see their stories re-created in animated form. Thanks to an enterprising film student named Daniel Kanemoto the whale story lives on in the glorious illustrated color of *Whalesong*. Of course, after seeing my likeness in the film, I'm not sure whether or not I should thank Mr. Kanemoto.

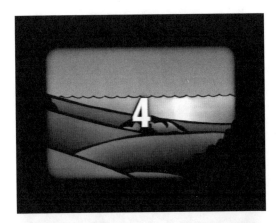

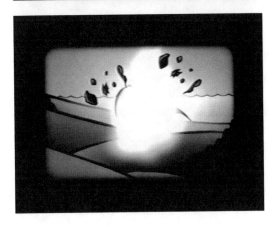

CHAPTER TWENTY-THREE

Who We Can Really Blame
for All of This

You can fool too many of the people
too much of the time.
—*James Thurber, "The Owl Who Was God," 1939*

ONE TIME I WAS COMPLAINING to another reporter about being weary of people writing and commenting to me about the whale, or worse, continually asking me where they could get a copy of it.

"If you really feel that way," my colleague said, "you ought to stop doing stories about it."

I didn't talk to the guy for a week; friends and coworkers who use honesty to stop you short like that should be avoided until they learn how to respond appropriately—commiserate and then bring up a work-related beef of their own.

And anyway, it wasn't my idea to keep doing such stories over the years; my producers insisted on it every time the anniversary date of the big blubber blast of 1970 rolled around. Do you think it was *my* idea to do a nine-part series when the quarter-century mark rolled around in 1995?

(Television news, incidentally, has always been big on anniversary pieces, especially in locations where there is not a lot of real news going on. It's a good way of filling up the nightly news hour, and explains why every year the newscast you watch does its requisite story on the big windstorm of 1962 or the fireworks factory explosion of whenever.)

Furthermore, I'm not the guy most responsible for perpetuating the whale story—or, for that matter, actually bringing it to the attention of millions of people outside of my own television station's viewing area. Nor am I the guy who works to this day to keep the story of the Big Blast of 1970 alive. That would be the celebrated syndicated columnist Dave Barry.

To give you an idea of what his motivation might be, I need only share something he said to me recently: "The exploding whale is the single funniest thing that I've ever seen." And trust me, this guy has seen a lot of funny things.

It was Barry, back in 1990, who first wrote about the subject for a mass audience. A couple of his readers had apparently sent him the video, and he loved it. He decided to give it his own unique spin in a column, which appeared on May 20, 1990, in the *Miami Herald* (and a few hundred other U.S. newspapers) under the heading, "Moby Yuck." (For those few of you who may have missed it, Barry's original story can be found at the end of this chapter.)

Unfortunately for me, it was also at about this time that a new phenomenon commonly called the Internet had discovered that it was easy to pirate just about anything with no qualms about crediting sources, let alone paying them. As noted earlier, the story of the exploding whale began appearing on a few sites; because its source was not revealed, it motivated many online readers to become exploding whale detectives. They would ultimately determine that the story had come from Barry, and that it was based on an actual incident.

"The reaction was pretty big," Barry recalls. "The immediate reaction was that I made it up, but then I started getting letters and calls from people who were there (when the whale exploded), or who claimed to be. The consensus was it was even more disgusting than you might think."

Dave Barry also writes books, and most likely because of the response to his column, he also put the whale in one of his best-sellers.

You'd think that would be enough, but apparently there's no stopping this man, because he's been out giving speeches about it, too.

"I just found people loved that story so much," he explains. "I've been talking about it for ten years or so, all across the country."

Dave Barry is not only very funny, he's a very good reporter. Upon reading his original story, and hearing him speak about the subject (which is but one of several quirky things he addresses in his public appearances), I realized at once that he had his facts right about the whale event. Well, I should note that in recounting what happened to Doug and me when all of that stuff started raining down on us on that fateful day, Barry at one point has it that "something smears the camera lens." That's not true, but listen, the man's a gifted storyteller and has the right to add his own little touches for, uh, flavor. I don't deny him that, and everything else he writes and says is right-on.

But since he'd had so much experience with the subject, I wanted to know what he thought it was that seems to captivate so many listeners, viewers, and readers about this odd little story.

"Most of the audiences I talk to have a lot of corporate types," he said. "They deal with making plans and carrying them out and they deal with government organizations. I think they kind of like the element that a large organization did something kind of insane because they've probably been part of something like it, or have been victimized by something similar."

Okay, that explains the corporate types' reaction. But what about, say, Dave Barry—why does he think it's so funny?

"Hey, Paul," he shouted, as if trying to get my attention. "It was a whale! There's just something about blowing up a whale. It's just an odd decision to make, and in the end, it's sort of wonderfully harmless. Nothing really terrible happened at anyone's expense."

Barry's got it right there, too. Even Walter Umenhofer is still laughing about getting his new car blubber-bombed.

Dave Barry says that when he first brings the subject up to his audience there is a slight murmur of recognition from some, but it's clear that about 95 percent of those present don't know where he's going with the subject. And at the end of his talks, when people come up to meet and congratulate him, they invariably ask the same question about the whale, whether he's in Pittsburgh or Pomona. They want to know where they can get a copy.

Fortunately—for me, and especially for Doug Brazil—Barry always tells them they can find it on the Internet by entering "Oregon's exploding whale" on their favorite search engine.

"And I always tell them," he concludes, "you'll find it funnier than I told it. I can't make it funnier than it actually is."

Moby Yuck
[Originally published May 20, 1990, in the *Miami Herald*]

Here at the Exploding Animal Research Institute we have received two very alarming news items that we are passing along today in the hopes that you, the generalized public, will finally break out of your apathetic, selfish, materialistic life styles and send us some large cash contributions.

Item One, submitted by numerous alert readers, concerns the recent criminally insane vote by the U.S. Senate AGAINST having the federal government monitor methane emissions from cows. I am not making this vote up. As you may be aware, cows emit huge quantities of methane, which contributes to global warming, which has gotten so bad in some areas that brand-new shirts are coming out of the factory with armpit stains already in them. So the U.S. Senate (motto: "White Male Millionaires Working for You") was considering an amendment to the Clean Air Act, under which the government would monitor methane emissions from various sources, including "animal production."

Well as you can imagine, this did not sit well with the senators from those states where cow flatulence is a cherished way of life. Leading the herd of opposition senators was Sen. Steve Symms of Idaho ("The Exploding Potato State"), who took the floor and stated that the amendment would—this is an actual quote—"put the nose of the federal government in almost every place it does not belong."

So the Senate took out the part about monitoring animal methane, which means there will be no advance warning when, inevitably, there is some kind of cow-interior blockage, causing a potentially lethal buildup of flammable gases and transforming one of these normally docile creatures into a giant mooing time bomb which, if detonated, could cause the dreaded Rain of Organs. Have you ever, in a supermarket, accidentally encountered a cow tongue—a large sluglike slab of gray flesh that you couldn't imagine anybody purchasing for any purpose other than to nail it to the front door in hopes of scaring off evil spirits? Well, I'd like to know what Sen. Symms would say if one of those babies came hurtling out of the sky and struck him at upwards of 100 miles per hour. "Yuck," would be my guess

I base this statement on a similar situation in Oregon where innocent civilians were struck by falling whale parts. I am absolutely not making this incident up; in fact, I have it all on videotape, which I obtained from the alert father-son team of Dean and Kurt Smith. The tape is from a local TV news show in Oregon, which sent a reporter out to cover a 45-foot, eight-ton dead whale that washed up on the beach. The responsibility for getting rid of the carcass was placed upon the Oregon State Highway Division, apparently on the theory that highways and whales are very similar in the sense of being large objects.

So anyway, the highway engineers hit upon the plan—remember, I am not making this up—of blowing up the whale with dynamite. The thinking here was that the whale would be blown into small pieces, which would be eaten by sea gulls, and that would be that. A textbook whale removal.

So they moved the spectators back up the beach, put a half-ton of dynamite next to the whale, and set it off. I am probably guilty of understatement when I say that what follows, on the videotape, is the most wonderful event in the history of the universe. First you see the whale carcass disappear in a huge blast of smoke and flame. Then you hear the happy spectators shouting "Yayy!" and "Wheee!" Then, suddenly, the crowd's tone changes. You hear a new sound, the sound of

many objects hitting the ground with noise that sounds like "splud."
You hear a woman's voice shouting "Here comes pieces of ... my GOD!"
Something smears the lens.

'   Later, the reporter explains: "The humor of the entire situation
suddenly gave way to a run for survival as huge chunks of whale
blubber fell everywhere." One piece caved in the roof of a car parked
more than a quarter of a mile away. Remaining on the beach were
several rotting whale sectors the size of condominium units. There was no
sign of the sea gulls, who had no doubt permanently relocated to Brazil.

This is a very sobering videotape. Here at the Institute we watch it
often, especially at parties. But this is no time for gaiety. This is a time
to get hold of the folks at the Oregon State Highway Division and ask
them, when they get done cleaning up the beaches, to give us an estimate
on the U.S. Capitol.

CHAPTER TWENTY-FOUR

Enough Is Enough

In plucking the fruit of memory one runs the risk
of spoiling its bloom.
—*Joseph Conrad,* Arrow of Gold, *1920*

I KNOW NOW that I will never completely escape the whale.

Not as long as I continue to hear from people who have their own anecdotes about the incident—including alleged relatives of the men who dynamited the beast, who insist that they have the "inside" story. Several others have written to say they were the insurance agent(s) who had to deal with Walter Umenhofer's crushed Oldsmobile. Many more didn't try to convince me that *they* were involved at all but that they *knew* someone who was. Of course, all of these good people are quite willing to share what "really" happened on that day in 1970.

Verifying any of their accounts would be impossible, even if I was so inclined, and for the most part, I have not done stories on these claimants.

I also never followed up on a few who informed me of other alleged whale disposal jobs, perhaps the most intriguing being the "whale of Livingston Mountain," which, as the story goes, swam hundreds of miles up the Columbia River before passing away in Washington State. There was no dynamite involved with that one, as far as I can tell.

And Florence isn't the only Oregon coastal city to blow up a whale, some writers insist; there were also bombastic blubber events in Newport and Cannon Beach and other places I can't recall. I've never seen convincing evidence of these events, but can't deny they may have happened.

Still another correspondent swore he knew of a motorist whose car was struck by flying blubber while traveling somewhere on Highway 101, nowhere near the time or the location of the exploding whale. Of course, the man who wrote me said he was the motorist's insurance agent.

If I were truly intent on keeping the exploding whale story alive, as some have suggested, I could do one such follow-up story weekly and never get to them all. I haven't and I won't.

All of these people who think I should be interested in their claims to the whale remind me of the first time I met Dave Barry. I was to interview him for a television talk show, and looked forward to it because I was certain he'd be thrilled to meet the reporter responsible for introducing one of his own favorite subjects.

But when we sat down in the studio, and I enthusiastically told him of my connection to the whale, he seemed completely underwhelmed by it. The conversation went fine, he gave me a very good interview, but I was troubled the entire time by his apparent lack of interest in the role I had played in what he would later term "the funniest thing I have ever seen."

Not long ago I spoke with him again for this project, and it became immediately clear to me why he had failed to react in the way I thought he might. The light went on when he told me about the many, many people who write, or approach him after his lectures, to inform him that they were actually present on the beach the day the whale was blown up. I had, in effect, become one of them when I met him, claiming not only to have been there but to have produced the video from which he wrote his column.

My estimate is that there were about seventy-five people, maximum, on the beach that day in 1970, yet Barry surely by now has encountered far more "eyewitnesses" than that, and I had unwittingly joined their number. Like the crowds that witnessed Willie Mays's catch or Bobby Thompson's home run, this one will never stop growing.

———————

Further, I have found that there will always be one more professional writer who will be compelled to take up the subject of the whale, some with historical perspective.

"A quarter of a century ago," wrote Zack Martin in *Electronic Media*, "Apollo 13 struggled to come back to Earth where the Beatles had just broken up. But in Florence, Oregon, that fall, citizens were transfixed by a momentous local event happening on their seashore."

Yet, for other writers, the whale provides the quintessential metaphor, for almost anything.

Writing on the state of broadcast news for the USC Annenberg *Online Journalism Review*, columnist Terry Anzur references the exploding whale in his lead, then makes this connection:

> *This explosive video clip of a 1970 incident on the Oregon Coast has been a popular download on the Web since 1994. And it's not a bad metaphor for the predicament facing broadcast journalists as more consumers turn to the Internet for news on demand. The whale on the beach is the traditional TV newscast and the receding waterline represents the shrinking broadcast audience.*

Okay, then! The article proceeds to chronicle a Radio-Television News Directors Association confab on the subject at the National Press Club in Washington, D.C., and concludes by returning to the metaphor:

> *The broadcast news whale is still on the cyber-beach and, at best, faces a treacherous swim in shark-infested Web waters.*

*The only thing we know for sure is that if it blows up, a huge,
untapped audience can watch on the Internet.*

I must admit that, when I first came upon this article, I found the
comparison to be quite a stretch, but I ended up liking it. If it's not a
good metaphor, I like the idea of the writer making the attempt right
out there for all of those professional journalists to see.

———————

Beyond the requests for video copies, I still regularly receive serious
inquiries about the whale from people who have seen the video or are
otherwise familiar with the story and who simply wish to know more
about it. Many ask how the state of Oregon presently handles the
disposal of dead whales.

The answer is that, where and when it's possible, they are not
disposed of at all. The thinking has long been that, environmentally,
it's best for all if nature is allowed to take its course. Unless they wash
up on beaches that are heavily used by the public, the dead whales are
simply left alone in most cases.

While the decision to make this standard practice, I am sure, had
nothing to do with what happened back in 1970, it's also true that state
officials haven't forgotten it.

"There's a strong institutional memory of that disaster," is the way
one put it to me.

But there are exceptions to the "leave them where they lie" idea.
In 1979, an amazing *forty-one* sperm whales washed up dead for
reasons unknown at one location, on a beach ironically not far
from the exploding whale site. State officials had them buried,
and erected a plaque to mark the location of this most unusual
occurrence.

I find this event to be infinitely more remarkable than the disposal
job of the single whale that I reported on nine years before, but who's
heard about it since? It's not all over the Internet, it didn't make *The*

World's Most Amazing Videos or an episode of *Family Law*. I mean, we're talking about a lot of dead whales here!

I guess because there was no dynamite used, no car crushed, no bystanders trying to escape cascading whale meat, it simply didn't garner the attention of that one ill-fated sperm whale.

And while I may be finished with it, I'm afraid the story will live on.

A friend told me recently that he had entered "Oregon's exploding whale" in his favorite Internet search engine and 86 pages of sites appeared, which he figured would reference about 850 specific sites. Not all of them contained downloadable versions, of course, but they did mention the phenomenon in one way or another. (I later had a niece tell me that that number is low. She insisted that her computer search for the exploding whale resulted in the identification of more than 1,200 sites!)

Many of these reference "chat rooms" in which the subject matter is discussed by Internet users, and entering one of them recently, it was all I could do to read the comments of those who were reacting to the video for the first time.

- *"I think this film is morbid and has no need to be on the internet,"* submitted Amber, who presented herself as a college student in Muncie, Indiana. *"To find humor in mutilating an animal, dead or alive, is frankly sickening and repulsive. If you have nothing better to do with your time than to make fun of and [sic] event that is so inhumane, you need to go and get yourself some psychological help."*
- *"I think it's funny as hell,"* reponded Dee from Colorado. *"Why be moralistic?"*
- *"Excellent,"* said Mark from Alberta.
- *"Who's the idiot who thought dynamite was the best thing to use?"* asked Steve from Rhode Island.
- *"Brilliant,"* chimed in Jo from London, *"only a bunch of bureaucrats could ever think it might work."*

• *"I think that what you did was highly imorral [sic],"* advised David from Oxfordshire in the United Kingdom.

On and on it went, for countless pages. I'm not sure why I found it so difficult to read their comments, but it definitely put me on edge.

Over the years, one of the trying aspects of the experience for me has been to become known as "the whale guy," not just among members of my television viewing audience but by many in my profession as well.

Following the broadcast of one of our "anniversary" reports on the whale, the Journalism Department at the University of Oregon invited me to debate a newspaper TV critic from Portland on the subject of whether our stories constituted good journalism or a cheap ratings ploy.

Honestly, I felt that there were good points on both sides, but my bottom line was that if people were still asking about it and clamoring for information decades after the fact—from us, the Internet, and the state of Oregon—it seemed almost as if we were obligated to report on it whenever its chronological milestones rolled around. Personally I would have preferred not to, but I could understand why the news organization I worked for was compelled to do so. And that's pretty much what I told the journalism students in Eugene.

My opponent's view was that it was nothing more than a shameless effort by a television station to increase its numbers. That rankled me, not so much because I disagreed with the claim, but because this was coming from a former TV anchorman turned columnist, who I felt should have enough experience to understand the broader view. (I'd seen his car in the lot upon arriving, and after hearing his comments, I pictured it in my mind with a big chunk of blubber flattening its roof and blowing out its windows.)

Members of the U of O faculty joined in the argument, too.

"It's a remarkable feature story," said assistant professor Al Stavitsky. I liked this guy, even before he added: "It's got danger, it's got drama. It's kind of quirky and it's sort of a 'foibles of science and government' kind of piece. It's a real good story."

Then, another view.

"You have to question," put forth professor Jim Upshaw, a former NBC correspondent, "if something like this on TV can drive out all of the other serious stuff you've handed them for ten or twenty minutes in a newscast. That's a critical issue which has do with what journalism is up to." Yeah? Well you can put that one on the viewing audience, not me, I thought. Our job is to present information, how the receiver prioritizes or processes it is out of the journalist's hands.

As I drove off campus, I couldn't help but wonder where Upshaw was parked.

It's much easier, I have found, to be the "whale guy" when visiting elementary school students. I still like to get together with young students to talk about writing, and to tell them about the fun they too could have if they should ever decide to become reporters. Somehow— I guess because they are just discovering the joys of a good story and storytelling—they relate to my little whale tale.

They listen with rapt attention, and then (at the urging of their teachers) write me letters, which contain their own drawings of the incident, and better, such thoughts as these:

"When the whale exploded did you have a lot of close [sic] on," wrote Nick, a second grader, "because if you didn't you would get a lot of blood on you."

"By coming here," wrote Sarah, "you have inspired me to add being a writer to my job list when I grow up."

"The exploding whale is funny," Peter wrote me. "I liked the part were the car got fatend [sic]."

But I guess my very favorite letter came from a second grader named Connor, and it manages to encapsulate in very few words the universal response to the exploding whale, what I've been hearing from so many people for so many years. It's a fitting end for our purposes here.

Connor had written me a very nice thank-you letter for visiting his class, complete with a globe he'd drawn with colored pencils at the bottom of the page, carrying the banner: "All Around the World." But then, it became apparent that he couldn't hold back what he really wanted to say any longer. Connor sought out the largest font possible on his computer to share what was in his heart, what he truly wanted— which is all that everyone else has apparently wanted from me as well. He wrote:

Please Send Us the Whale Tape

I like the way Connor put it. His writing is spare, honest, and to the point. Most of my whale correspondents over the years needed several paragraphs to accomplish what he did in six words. Like my English teacher told me years ago, I think Connor can write a little, and maybe he should think about a journalism career.

It's certainly been a wonderful and curious journey for me, one that has included the exploding whale, in one way or another, most of the way. This book feels like the last chapter of that story; I've shared just about everything anyone might want to know about it. If the urban legend is destined to live on in some way I can't imagine, it will require a new storyteller.

And to be honest, when all is said and done, I am grateful fate involved me in a tale that's proved to be of such universal fascination. I may not completely understand why so many people have been so interested for so long, but must admit it's been fun keeping track of a story that simply refused to die.

It's also served as a measure by which I've watched my years as a reporter fly by. Oddly, in certain ways, I still consider myself a beginner who is trying to learn his craft, hoping each time out that somehow the audience will be as thrilled with the story as the storyteller is. Journalism, perhaps more than any other endeavor, seems to be something you learn by doing, and I now understand it's a never-ending pursuit. There will always be yet another inspirational person to meet, another great story to tell.

And if you're lucky, one that will never go away.

ACKNOWLEDGMENTS

THIS BOOK WOULDN'T HAVE HAPPENED and the exploding whale story would not have been so widely told had it not been for the original camera work of Doug Brazil. I am grateful for his friendship over the years, and for his assistance on the book project. Doug coordinated the graphics—shepherding television scenes onto the printed page—and was invaluable in helping me recall certain facts and details. The whale never made us wealthy, but it gave us something we could share, ruminate on, and laugh about forever, and that's worth quite a bit.

KATU Television, the ABC affiliate station in Portland, owned by Fisher Communications, has been my professional home almost continuously since 1968. I'm appreciative that the management and staff were so supportive of my journalistic efforts, allowing me to bring thousands of worthy people to the attention of our nightly news audiences when there was certainly more "important" news that needed to be squeezed in. I don't know of many places that would allow a reporter to do more than twelve hundred stories on good people doing good things—this one did. Oh yes, and also the whale story, time and time again!

Ed Schoaps at the Oregon Department of Transportation has gone above and beyond the call of duty in responding to inquiries on the exploding whale, and was also of great help in the research of this book. Many thanks to Ed, and to his colleague Ted Burney in ODOT's archives department, who himself has sent out hundreds of dubs of the exploding whale story. Thanks, too, to Dr. Bruce Mate at the Oregon State University Marine Science Center for helping me understand more about the whales that migrate past my home state twice a year, especially the one that came to such an infamous end.

My colleagues at Graphic Arts Center Publishing have been extremely supportive of me through two book projects. Many thanks to my friend and publisher Mike Hopkins, who has been a help to me professionally and personally, and to associate publisher Doug Pfeiffer. Their backing has meant more than I can say. Tim Frew, my editor, has done a wonderful job of keeping this project on track and in helping me make sense of a great deal of disparate information. Tim never failed to raise the right question or seek clarification where it was needed, plus I always knew I could count on him for early morning golf, where the book's major problems could be resolved. I'm grateful to Juli Warner, marketing guru, for seeing that this quirky little story received the most attention possible, and for being just as thrilled as everyone else the first time she saw the video.

I especially appreciate Dave Barry's involvement in the project. Dave once said that he felt he "owed" me for letting him have so much fun with this story, but I am truly in his debt for doing more than anyone to keep it alive. Either that or I should blame him for it—I'm not quite sure which!

Thanks to the thousands of people who made contact with us to express interest in the exploding whale, and to the thousands of feature subjects who taught me so much as I captured their personal stories for the evening news. Both groups have added immeasurably to my professional life.

Finally, and most importantly, I am most grateful for my wife, Vicki, who was my first reader and editor on this book. She helped mightily with every single page, no easy task considering that she's heard all of these stories many, many times before. I will never be able to thank her enough.